Best
Shropshire Walks

Les Lumsdon

First edition printed 1996
Reprinted with revisions 2000, 2005, 2007

Second edition printed 2010

Published by Sigma Leisure – an imprint of
Sigma Press, Stobart House, Pontyclerc, Penybanc Road
Ammanford, Carmarthenshire SA18 3HP

British Library Cataloguing in Publication Data

A CIP record for this book is available from the British Library

ISBN: 978-1-85058-853-5

Typesetting and Design by: Sigma Press, Ammanford, Carms

Maps: Bute Cartographics

Photographs: Chloë Lumsdon

Printed by: Cromwell Press Group, Trowbrige, Wiltshire

Disclaimer: The information in this book is given in good faith and is believed to be correct at the time of publication. Care should always be taken when walking in hill country. Where appropriate, attention has been drawn to matters of safety. The author and publisher cannot take responsibility for any accidents or injury incurred whilst following these walks. Only you can judge your own fitness, competence and experience. Do not rely solely on sketch maps for navigation: we strongly recommend the use of appropriate Ordnance Survey (or equivalent) maps.

Contents

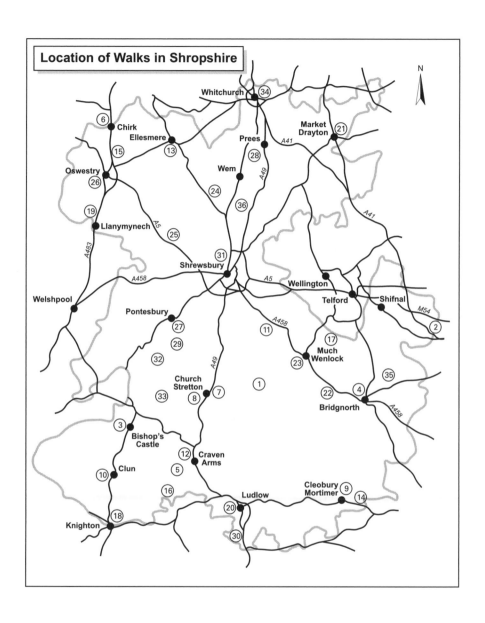

Location of Walks in Shropshire

N

Rail Ramblers waiting for the Heart of Wales train

The Subtle Beauty of Shropshire

Of the border counties Shropshire holds the greatest promise for the walker. From wild, heather hills and wooded scarps to gentle riverside paths and green lanes once trodden by travelling folk, the subtle beauty of the Shropshire landscape begins to unfold.

The Epitome of England

Enticing though the Shropshire Hills may be, the County offers far more. It is, after all, the largest inland county (now a unitary authority known as Shropshire Council) and stretches from a point south of Ludlow virtually to the Potteries and from the fringes of the West Midlands conurbation to the western slopes of Clun Forest. Within this administrative area there is a rich variety of landscapes, a point so eloquently made by an editor of the well-respected *Murray's Travel Companion* in the late 1870s:

> *'Salop can be considered an epitome of England, for it contains within the compass of a few miles all the characteristics of an Alpine district in miniature, while at the same time within sight of orchards, gardens and farmhouses.'*

Could we say different now? Despite the increase in traffic on main roads and additional housing at the periphery of villages and towns, there still remains a rurality about the county which is more precious than many of us openly admit. The landscape within the Shropshire Hills Area of Outstanding Natural Beauty (AONB) is of particular importance and many a walker is grateful for its existence.

The Great Divider

The Severn is a great divider. Roughly speaking the land area to the north is a gently undulating plain, but not without highlights. The underlying rock is mainly new red sandstone and those little ridges such as Harmer, Grinshill and Weston offer fine viewpoints across a seemingly endless plain. Of course, The Wrekin (actually situated in adjacent Telford and Wrekin) is something special. Although not that high (1334 feet), it is a very distinctive landmark which people genuinely cherish; it remains part of the cultural discourse to this day. It is a break point between the plain and the Severn itself as it makes its way through the Ironbridge Gorge.

This gives out to Bridgnorth and the Wyre Forest with pockets of ancient woodland intersected by lesser known tributaries such as the Dowles and Mor brooks and the Worfe. There are pockets of mixed farming, parkland, orchards and dairying too.

Meres

The north west of the county is special in a different way; it is characterised by meres and gently undulating hills. These natural lakes, brought about in post-glacial times when large flows of melting ice gouged out hollows and deposited in return clayey layers, are welcome retreats for wildlife and offer opportunities for short strolls for the rambler. Hence the area is often referred to as 'The Little Lakeland of Shropshire'.

West of Oswestry

To the west of Oswestry, however, the landscape becomes far more dramatic with high ground and plunging valleys, indistinguishable from Wales, marked only by occasional road signs and the centuries old Offa's Dyke. This is borderland and is rich in landscape and heritage and the book includes a walk on Wat's Dyke to the Old Fort at Oswestry as well as on Offa's Dyke itself.

South of The Severn

South of the Severn, the landscape is more varied. Not only do you find the delightful valleys of the Corve, Rea, Onny and Teme but also more undulating farmland sweeping away from the Clee Hills, the Wyre Forest and wooded edges such as at Benthall and its more famous counterpart, Wenlock Edge; they make for superb rambles.

Shropshire Hills AONB

Returning to the south west of the county, it is in this part that the highest hills are to be found. The Long Mynd is well known to many and Caradoc, the Lawley, and Ragleth are much loved by the rambler. But move west towards Clun Forest and this isolated sheep farming country offers a solitude rarely found elsewhere in the Midlands. A mile or so away from the 'honeypot' areas and you are off the beaten track. It is wild country and long may we conserve it.

Stay Awhile

These introductory comments offer no more than the briefest sketch, a whetting of the appetite to discover this delightful part of England. In such a short space, it would be impossible to capture the unsophisticated charm of Shropshire country life exhibited in local farming, crafts, village events and town markets. Walking, after all, is not just about notching up mile after mile, it is about gaining a feeling for the landscape, staying awhile at a village inn, or local café, and talking to people who live and work in the countryside. The visit becomes so much more enjoyable and especially if you stay for a night or two in the area where you are walking. You can relax and get to know a place more without rushing around in a car. These words were first penned over twenty years ago but they could not be more apposite now; for the terms slow travel and low carbon tourism have entered our 21st century vocabulary and will be key words of the coming decades. The appeal of travelling at a pace where you can see and hear wildlife, smell wild flowers and take time to appraise the landscape has much to commend it. Perhaps, more importantly, it is also far less impacting on the environment; we can leave it in good order for future generations. And there are local companies like Wheely Wonderful Cycling and Walking who have superb short break slow travel packages to hand.

Shropshire's Other Attractions

As well as the countryside, Shropshire has a number of visitor attractions from Ludlow and its Castle to the much loved Severn Valley Railway. On the border of Telford and Wrekin is the World Heritage Centre Site, Ironbridge, set in the Ironbridge Gorge. In Shrewsbury there are several attractions including Shrewsbury Abbey upon which the fictional medieval monk, Brother Cadfael was partly based. To the north is Hawksworth Park, Victorian gardens and monuments used in the filming of The Chronicles of Narnia screened on television in previous years.

It is not only the formal attractions. There's nothing better than coming across an open day or village carnival when you are on your ramble. Most of the walks start from a village or town and many of these are very attractive in their own right.

Wayside Curiosities

On your travels, look out for many vernacular features such as the corrugated barn, old ironwork associated with parklands, village pounds, and suchlike. There are

Vernacular architecture

also many wayside curiosities, the whipping posts at Morville, the unique ferry crossing at Hampton Loade, the milestones and high arched bridges on the Shropshire Union Canal or the mining relics at Snailbeach. A favourite of mine is the water trough which used to stand behind the Craven Arms Hotel and now sits less ceremoniously on the main A49 road. It has the inscription: 'Be Kind and Merciful to Animals' although the trough itself has been concreted over.

The Taste of Shropshire

Many farms are now turning to grow and process local speciality products and Shropshire is fortunate to enjoy these. Maynards, Tudges and Walls sausages, for example, are some of the finest in the country. These local companies offer food which has been farmed and cured near to where it is sold. The exquisite farmhouse cheeses from near Newport and Whitchurch are to be found in the Farmers Market. There are a wide range of Shropshire products on offer from rapeseed oil, honey and oatmeal

Winter wassail of an orchard

biscuits to fruit and vegetables in local shops. Ludlow is also an area renowned for slow food, where good local products are prepared without haste.

Unlike its neighbour (Herefordshire), Shropshire has never been a big producer of cider, although Mahorall is now firmly in the local market. There are also three vineyards which come to mind: Halpenny Green, Ludlow (Clee St Margaret) and Wroxeter. However, the major development has been the rise of small scale independent breweries in the county: All Nations at Madeley, Bridgnorth Brewery, Corvedale at Corfton, Hobsons at Cleobury Mortimer, Ludlow Brewery, Salopian at Shrewsbury, Six Bells at Bishop's Castle, Stonebridge at Oswestry, Three Tuns Shropshire Brewery at Bishop's Castle, the Wem Brewing Company, Wood at Wistanstow, and Worfield (Ironbridge)at The All Nations, Madeley. Each brewer produces a distinctive style of beer and what a choice. There are other pub breweries too. Long live the traditional beverages championed by the Campaign For Real Ale!

Country Pubs

Everyone likes a country pub, and Shropshire has managed to retain dozens of them. Many have survived in the isolated places and others have retained a strong local village trade over the decades. But we have lost many in the last decade too; this is an erosion of the local rural economy. Having tried many hostelries mentioned on route (for quality control purposes, of course!), it has been a pleasure to meet so many interesting landlords and landladies who love their communities and the countryside.

Most pubs welcome walkers, but times have changed and gone are many of the bars which were built to serve the farm worker. In order to survive, country inns have moved more towards providing accommodation and serving food. Generally speaking, many have retained their character, which makes a break for a pint and a meal a real pleasure. Children are almost always welcome at lunchtimes and early evenings (if they are not over boisterous) and there is outdoor seating at most places for warmer weather.

Publicans tend to dislike boots if they are muddy, heavy rucksacks placed in dangerous locations, people eating their own food and are in the main not able to accept dogs inside. So please bear these factors in mind before you step in.

The Three Horseshoes at Bridges

Opening hours are always a problem to report as there is no consistent pattern. Lunchtime opening seems to continue until about 3.00pm, depending on custom at most places, with early opening on Summer evenings from 6.00pm onwards. Saturday is a better day, with more pubs staying open throughout. Sunday lunchtime hours are generally maintained through until 3.00 or 4.00pm. Monday is the worst day in that many pubs are closed Monday lunchtimes. It is difficult to be more precise.

Pubs can make a country walk, so enjoy a stop en route or at the end of a ramble.

Long Distance Paths

Shropshire is host to a number of long distance paths including The Severn Way, The Shropshire Way and The Offa's Dyke Path and The Mortimer Trail from Ludlow through to Kington in Herefordshire. Offa's Dyke is a favourite. Of its 142 miles some of the best stretches straddle Shropshire. From the small town of Montgomery in Powys to the border town of Knighton, the path winds its way between Wales and Shropshire crossing The Kerry Ridgeway into the tranquil valley of the Unk and onto Churchtown and then Newcastle. Some of the finest earthworks are to be found between Newcastle and Knighton. The Shropshire Way offers a circular walk, with optional sections, around the County; it has been upgraded in recent years. The route is as varied as the county itself and traverses paths and bridleways throughout with very little road walking. It came into existence through the good work of a number of rambling groups including several local branches of the Ramblers' Association in consultation with the County Council. The route can be either accomplished on a walking holiday or as a series of walks between towns and villages on the main loop. In recent years the Shropshire Way has been upgraded and it is best to google 'Shropshire Walking' for the latest news.

The Mortimer Trail is an exquisite route through lands once ruled over by the Mortimer family, hence the name. The 30 mile route follows a series of ridges between Ludlow and Kington offering exceptional views and real seclusion. There are many other long distance paths skirting the county and several are included in the book.

The Walks

There are 36 walks featured in the book covering most parts of Shropshire from the deepest rural enclaves around Clun to settlements borne of early industrialisation. Inevitably, some sections have been written up in recent years in other walks but there are over 12 new walks in this edition.

The Horse Shoe Inn at Bridges

Information

The walks are from three to eleven miles in length and vary from easy going to fairly strenuous. Essential information is supplied at the beginning of each walk. In this way, for example, you can decide whether you wish to go for an easy ramble, visit a pub, call in at an attraction, etcetera. On the other hand, if you are looking for a moderately strenuous four to six hours walk then you'll find these too. The choice is yours.

Family Walks

Many of the walks are suitable for families with younger children. Take, for example, the walk at Yorton or in the Wyre Forest. They are ideal for families seeking a short ramble and an opportunity to move on to a local attraction. In fact, most of the walks can be adapted as they have cut-off points allowing shorter rambles for little legs.

Travel

All of the walks have been selected so as to allow access by public transport; this is part of the slow travel way of things. There's no hassle with parking, or the security of vehicles in isolated places and driving down back lanes. The train tends to be universally popular and Rail Rambles are a testament to the vision of the late Alan Howard and others who have since managed to produce thousands of rail based walks over the past twenty plus years. Thus, several of the walks are specifically written up to include a rail or bus journey. For example, the Knighton to Bucknell or Hopton Heath to Craven Arms walks use the Heart of Wales line and the Prees to Wem ramble offers more diversity as a linear walk from the Crewe line. They can be walked on Sundays too as the train service is daily. The 'Shropshire Hills Shuttles' have been much loved by walkers (see website in factfile section) and I commend them to you for many of the walks such as Bishop's Castle, Clun, Stiperstones and Wentnor. People who have reached that marvellous age, where they are entitled to free bus travel, will find this book very useful too. Using the bus is great on the pocket and even better for the environment so why not give it a try. Admittedly, some places are difficult to get to by public transport; Acton Burnell is perhaps the hardest to reach in the book. On the other hand, many of the walks are served by bus or train every day of the week.

Maps

The walks should be easy to follow simply by using the instructions in the book. Some readers will want, however, to use a map in conjunction with the book. The Ordnance Survey maps 1: 50,000 scale Landranger Maps covering the area are adequate but far better for walking are the OS Explorer 1: 25,000 scale maps. The relevant ones are listed for each walk. They can be helpful when studying the lie of the land, the field patterns, the direction of streams and so on.

The Landrangers are, however, excellent for finding your way around the county. The key maps required are:

Kidderminster and Wyre Forest – Sheet 138
Ludlow and Wenlock Edge – Sheet 137
Shrewsbury – Sheet 126
Stafford, Telford and surrounding area – Sheet 127

Directions

The suggested walking times provided in the text are merely for guidance. If you like a paced walk then the times provided will be over generous, but if you are out to saunter awhile then they'll not be far wrong. Virtually all of the walks involve climbing stiles of some description. Directions are given assuming your back is to the stile every time you cross a field boundary. The County Council often provides waymark roundels on stiles which is helpful.

Changing Environment

It goes without saying that there will be change. After all, it is a working landscape crafted mainly by the farming community. Crops will be rotated, barns converted and trees planted where grass was once sown. Sometimes walks become a little overgrown, even when a number of us walk them throughout the year and a stick can come in handy on such occasions (also for streams and warding off animals). It is likely that some paths and bridleways will be improved since they were first researched for this publication. In other instances, there might even be minor diversions and alterations to the route. Wherever possible these are usually signed and easy to follow back to the original route. I can only apologise for such things in advance but common sense, no doubt, will prevail when you are on the walk.

A few matters do concern people when they're out in the countryside especially when they are not used to walking in an area of mixed farming. People sometimes hesitate when they find that a crop has been planted and the path not reinstated. Rights of way are literally what they mean. You are entitled to walk without obstruction whether it be a crop or other impediment along the way. Thus, you should keep to that way and tread a path accordingly. That is the law.

Although the regulations allow some bulls in fields crossed by rights of ways it is best to walk as far away as possible to them. Cows can be a little frisky in winter months when they think you are bringing them food but generally do not cause concern. In areas of grazing, fields are sometimes cordoned off by low level electric fencing which gives a mild shock to animal and human alike so step over them gingerly; it is a constant source of frustration to walkers.

Any serious obstructions, however, should be brought to the attention of the Rights of Way section at Shropshire Council. It is only by our reporting such matters that we save other walkers from difficulties.

We sometimes forget though that it is a working countryside so expect to come across lanes which are sometimes used by herds of cows in wet weather and hence can become very muddy. In fact, most paths are likely to be muddy after rain so it is better to wear stout footwear – boots or Wellingtons. It is also essential to carry rainwear. On the hills it is vital that you wear proper windproof and waterproof garments in case the weather turns. A small amount of food and a first aid kit, compass and torch can be tucked into a rucksack without any discomfort.

Shropshire is a splendid county; the rights of way network has improved immeasurably thanks to the rights of way team and the many groups, such as the Ramblers and Parish Paths Partnerships, which have put in much good work to upgrade paths and bridleways so they are passable. Hats off to all of those involved. This book introduces you to some walks which would not have been possible, even a decade ago. It also includes the timeless classics of Caradoc, The Long Mynd and The Stiperstones. As I said twenty years ago, Shropshire is a most promising county for the walker. In my book, it still is.

Factfile
Here are some useful contacts:

Public Transport
National Rail Enquiries: 08457 48 49 50
Shropshire Hills Shuttle: www.shropshirehillsshuttles.co.uk
Train Tracker: up to the minute information on departing trains from stations: 0871 200 49 50
Traveline: provides information on buses on 0871 200 22 33

Rights of Way
If you come across any obstructions then please contact the Shropshire Council rights of way team:
Countysideaccess@shropshire.gov.uk
Or telephone 01743 25501

Walking Organisations
Long Distance Walkers Assocation: www. ldwa.org.uk
Ramblers: www.ramblers.org or telephone 020 7339 8500

Walking Holidays
Secret Hills Walking: alangarner@wsol.co.uk or telephone Alan Garner on 01694 723600

Wheely Wonderful Cycling and Walking Holidays:
info@wheelywonderfulcycling.co.uk or telephone Kay or Chris Dartnell on 01568 770755

1. Acton Burnell

Easy walking for those who love history for this walk takes in Acton Burnell Castle and Langley Chapel, both of which are managed by English Heritage.

Distance	**3 miles (5km) or 4 miles (6-7km) if you visit Langley Chapel**
Allow	**2 hours walking time**
Map	**OS Explorer 241 Shrewsbury**
By bus	**The 540 bus from Shrewsbury to Cardington calls at Acton Burnell Post Office; the best day of travel is Saturday with an outward or return journey on the 435 bus to Leebotwood where you change to or from the 540 bus**
By car	**From Shrewsbury by way of the A49 to Bayston Hill, then left to Condover, another left and right turn to Frodesley. From there it is another left to Acton Burnell. Alternatively, travel on the A458 to Weeping Cross where you turn off right to Pitchford and Acton Burnell by way of Cantlop Bridge. There's a small amount of parking near to Acton Burnell Castle**
Refreshments	**There is a shop and Post Office on Frodesley Road in the village**
Nearest Tourist Information Office	**Visitor Information Centre, Rowley's House, Barker Street Tel: 01743 281200 visitorinfo@shropshire.gov.uk**

Acton Burnell castle, now in the hands of English Heritage, is open to the public at any reasonable hour. It comes as something of a disappointment to those expecting a lumbering, great motte and bailey for Acton Burnell was never a castle as such; it was fortified manor. This castle was built in the late 13th century, more as a residence than a fortress. The owner, Robert Burnell, the Bishop of Bath and Wells, had to apply to the monarch for a special licence to make it look like a mock castle as in those days you required an early-day version of outline planning permission to do such things.

Behind the ruins of the castle stand two end gables of an earlier building referred to as 'The Parliamentary Barn'. It is thought that Edward I called a Parliament of sorts here to enact a piece of legislation to make notable debtors pay up to the monarchy within a given time limit. Beyond the ruins is the elegant hall, now a college, with its grand Georgian frontage, a style of design much favoured by affluent landowners of the 18th century. Do not miss the church, situated close to the castle, as it has some fine effigies of Sir Richard Lee and Sir Humphrey Lee, forefathers of Robert E Lee of Wild West fame. Steal yourself away from these fine buildings of antiquity for a while to enjoy a short ramble with views over to Frodesley Lodge and The Lawley.

1. Start the walk at the Post Office on Frodesley Road. From the entrance turn left and keep ahead at the cross roads towards the private college. Just before reaching the college gates, turn right on the access road to

The church and castle at Acton Burnell

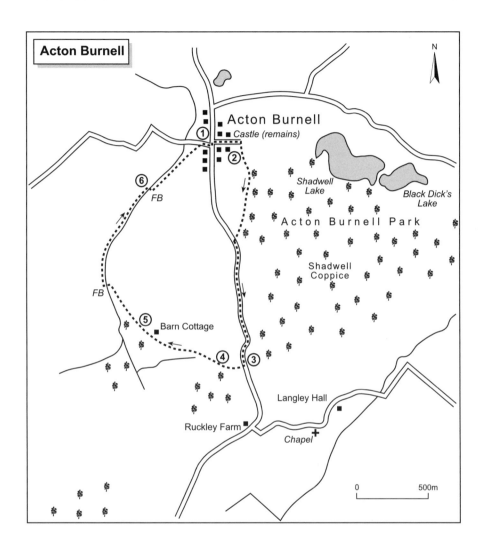

the ruins of Acton Burnell Castle. Go through the access gate in the top right corner of the wooded area adjoining the church and castle to join the path which leads to the Ruckley Road.

2. Once through the kissing gate, go left and continue alongside the wall boundary of Acton Burnell Park over stiles until you come out at a road. There's a superb view of the Lawley from this vantage point. Go

The fortified castle at Acton Burnell

left and follow this road for a good half mile until you approach Ballshill Cottage on the left. Look for a gate on the right opposite the drive.

3. However, pause a while. You may like to visit Langley Chapel, which is just under a half mile away by road. Continue ahead on the road to Ruckley hamlet where you turn left. Langley Chapel is located on the right before the serene Langley Hall. Access to the chapel is available between 10-17.00 hours every day from the start of March until the end of November. Nearby is the restored 15th century gatehouse belonging to a much larger medieval settlement known as Langley Hall. This is a private residence not open to the public. Retrace your steps back to Ballshill.

4. Go through the barred gate (now on your left) as signposted. Walk alongside the field boundary to your left into the next field by way of a gap in the hedge. Go slightly right to a gate. Keep to the left of the derelict cottage.

5. You reach a cross-roads of bridleways at a point almost parallel with the derelict building. Keep ahead here and follow the wood's edge. As the fence drops away to the left, proceed ahead to go through a gateway. A short way along this hedge, look for a footbridge on the left. Go over it and then turn right, following the stream in the shallow valley where you keep ahead to cross two stiles. There has been a considerable amount of work done to improve wildlife habitats here. You eventually come to a replanted pocket of trees and a footbridge on the right.

6. Cross it and go left following the hedge to the corner and then along the rear of a garden where you will find a stile. Go left over it. Do not be put off by the fencing; this is to protect the hens in the small strip of land through which you now pass. Cross a stile and drop down to the road. Go right to walk back into the village. What a pleasant interlude in a quiet corner of Shropshire.

2. Albrighton to Shifnal

Easy walking along roads and tracks followed by paths through a delightful valley to Shifnal. There's a real contrast on the walk between intensive farming (taking in part of Monarch's Way) and pastoral England.

Distance	10 miles (16km)
Allow	5 hours
Map	OS Explorer 242 Telford, Ironbridge and The Wrekin
By train	There is an hourly service from Wolverhampton, Shrewsbury and Telford, daily, which stops at Albrighton and Shifnal
By bus	The 890/2 bus runs daily between the Telford and Wolverhampton calling at both towns en route
By car	Travel on the A41 and then A464 from Wolverhampton or on the latter from Telford. Travel by way of the A442, B4379 and A4169 from Bridgnorth
Refreshments	There are pubs and shops in Albrighton and Shifnal. There is also a pub which welcomes walkers, The Seven Stars, in Beckbury
Nearest Tourist Information Office	Telford shopping centre Tel: 01952 291723 tourist-info@telfordshopping.co.uk

Albrighton is a small dormitory town for the West Midlands and is situated near to the Royal Air Force Museum at Cosford. Shifnal grew up as a coaching town on the route through to Wales and Ireland. Inns such as the Jerningham Arms were busy places with coaches calling in at all manner of times. In the 19th century the first to call would have been 'The Wonder' at 6.30 am from Shrewsbury. A change of horses, a quaff of ale and away it went. The inns are still busy but the coaches have gone. The railways put paid to their trade in the last century but the legacy of the past is still evident in the townscape.

1. This is a linear walk so you need to travel by train or bus between Shifnal and Albrighton or travel there entirely by public transport. Start the walk at Albrighton railway station. Walk down the station entrance into Station Road and go left. At the main junction, turn right along High Street. Part way along, opposite the churchyard, turn left into Church Road. Pass Grange Road and just before a shop on the left turn right along a drive to a narrow path between gardens through to Bowling Green Lane. Go left and on reaching the roundabout go ahead to leave the urban quarter behind.

2. This attractive lane is spoilt only by the traffic; it is easy to see the damage done to the old hedgerows by vehicles inching past each other so be wary. You pass the entrance to David Austin Roses, famous for the cultivation of roses which came into fashion in Victorian times. Eventually you reach the main A464 road which you cross and join a quieter lane wandering through flat land which made it possible for RAF Cosford to be built. This lane is also the route chosen for Monarch's Way, which you will follow through to Beckbury. Monarch's Way (615 miles of it!) focuses on the journey of King Charles II when fleeing from the Parliamentarian troops after being routed at the Battle of Worcester in 1651. The good king (discuss) took refuge in many homesteads and villages throughout the land and seemingly had a habit of hiding in old oak trees. Well, we have all heard that one before. But the most recited example is at Bobscobel (north of Albrighton); it is impressive. There are several oaks on this lane that would do the job, but it would be lovely to see more planted.

3. The road bends to the right and left and here you get your first chance to walk on terra firma as the road bends left. Go diagonally across the field towards a dwelling. Exit at the corner by an electric telegraph pole. So, it is back on the road and no doubt sooner than you expected. Keep ahead to the next corner by Cayton Cottages. Go ahead along a

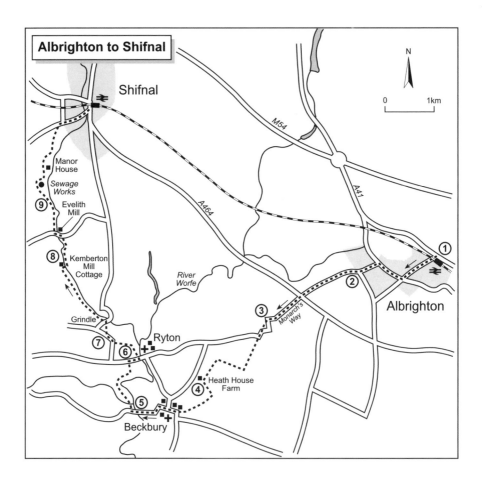

concrete track; there's variation in this walk. This bends right and left to pass a dwelling and Heath House Farm. It is interesting to contrast the endless prairie style cultivation (no hedges, landmarks or trees) with the pastures to be walked in an hour or so.

4. At the farm you reach a crossroads. Go ahead and mid way along the drive go slightly right across the field at a way-mark post aiming for Beckbury village; it is usually an arable crop but a request has gone in for re-instatement of the path each year. As you get closer to the houses you will see an opening in the hedgerow. Go down this 'lost way' to join a road in the village. Keep ahead on the road to pass the

church on your left. Ignore the turning on the right in this picture postcard village, but keep ahead as the road winds its way past the Seven Stars pub and across the River Worfe.

5. Rise up to a corner, with a dwelling on your left, to cross a stile on the right. Head slightly right to walk over a footbridge. Once you are over, aim slightly left to join fencing which curves to the left. Follow this to climb steadily up the bluff and to a stile. Climb over the stile and go right to walk along the bluff and where fencing meets a hedge cross a stile and go left along a hedge (now to your left). You reach the corner of the field at the top of a dry valley and walk alongside a hedge until you come to a barred gate on your left. Go through here and follow the track to the road.

6. The road descends and bends left. Opposite the telephone kiosk go left along a path between dwellings, past a community hall, and into a field. Keep ahead but climb the bank and move closer to the hedge on the left. You see across the valley the outline of Ryton church and hall. Part way along the hedge cross a stile on the left and now follow another hedge on your left to the hamlet of Grindle. The path exits by a barred gate on to the road.

7. Go right and walk by the houses of Grindle to a corner where there's another group of houses. Opposite the telephone kiosk (déjà vu) go left over a stile by a house and walk alongside the garden to another stile which you cross. Go ahead to climb another stile and you now have a wonderful view of Grindle Forge below. Walk alongside the hedge down to the road. Go right and before reaching the bridge go left, as signposted on the edge of a drive and garage, to a little path which meanders through the wood, over a stile, and then near to the Wensley Brook to climb up to a stile in the far corner of the pasture. Go over it and proceed ahead through woodland, dipping in a gully and then up to cross a stile. Keep ahead along the fencing and another stile. Proceed onward through old hawthorns but keep more or less the same contour rather than descending closer to the stream. You cross a stile and now descend to walk towards a cottage and old buildings, presumably part of an old mill complex. Cross a stile and walk alongside the garden and cottage to reach a drive. Go right here to skirt an old brick building and the path crosses two footbridges to a junction. Think back to one hour ago.

8. Go left and walk along a track through King Charles Wood, festooned with bluebells in the Spring. It becomes a path running ahead to Evelith Mill. It is hard to believe that this little brook powered so many mills in the valley. At the road go left, cross the bridge and ignore the path on the right along the drive. However, once over the bridge look for a path on the right through a pocket of woodland. Keep more or less ahead, crossing two stiles as you progress up the valley. The path eventually nears the stream and becomes wetter. It reaches a footbridge. Do not cross it. Instead, go up the track to a junction.

9. Turn right here and before the security fencing turn left on a concrete road and then immediately right to walk on a path which skirts the sewerage works. Go through a kissing gate and ahead up the bank. The path runs alongside fencing to the left of dwellings and joins a track where you go left. This reaches the main road where you turn right for a short pavement section to Shifnal. At the corner, go ahead up Church Street, past St Andrews church and onto the High Street. Cross over for access to Shifnal railway station.

3. Bishop's Castle

A delightful short ramble for those wishing to walk off a lunch served in one of Bishop's Castle's fine hostelries. Easy walking with more downhill sections than climbs!

Distance	3½ miles (5.5km)
Allow	2 hours
Map	OS Explorer 216 Welshpool and Montgomery
By bus	There is a regular daily service 552/3 from Shrewsbury and a less frequent service from Ludlow and Craven Arms on Mondays, Thursday and Fridays only. The Shropshire Hills Shuttle allows access via Craven Arms on Saturdays and Sundays from April to the end of September
By car	Bishop's Castle is just off the A488 from Shrewsbury or the A489 from Craven Arms. There is a public car park near to the livestock market in Station Street
Refreshments	There are inns, cafés and shops offering refreshment in Bishop's Castle
Nearest Tourist Information Office	Old Time, High Street, Bishop's Castle Tel: 01588 638467 jane@oldtime.co.uk

The *Town Trail* booklet invites you to look down High Street from The Market Square and imagine the town in earlier times, for Bishop's Castle retains a layout planned in the twelfth century. The castle once stood at the top of the town, behind where The Castle Hotel is now situated (and what a superb pub garden) and looked over a main thoroughfare running down to the church at the bottom of the town. A series of much smaller

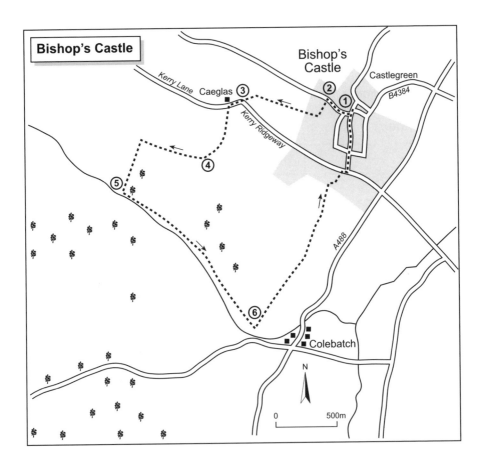

lanes crosses this main street to complete the grid.

While standing in this vicinity take a look down Salop Street at the Three Tuns brewery and public house, dating from times when most public houses brewed their own. The brewery is a sturdy survivor having lived through the recent decades of large scale brewery mergers. It has had several owners in recent years but continues to brew fine ales. At the other end of the town is the much loved Six Bells brewery.

Bishop's Castle has always been a significant borderland township, with markets attracting both English and Welsh over the centuries. It was at one time the smallest borough in England, known as a Rotten Borough in that its limited population did not really warrant two members of Parliament. Ironically, in 1820 all four candidates in the election polled a mere 87 votes each and in the absence of any other procedure they were all duly elected! From 1832 onwards the political status of Bishop's Castle has declined considerably.

Of all the Shropshire railway lines the Bishop's Castle railway must have been the most impecunious. Built in the 1860s this railway was doomed from the beginning. The hopes of driving a 'road' through to Montgomery and into Mid Wales were not realised and a track from Craven Arms to Bishop's Castle could never make commercial sense even in the days before cars. Consequently, of its 70 years' existence, 69 of them were in the hands of the receiver! There are dozens of yarns about the line and even to this day it is referred to with great affection.

Bishop's Castle is a good place to stay for a few days as it is a Walkers are Welcome town. Pick up the *Town Trail* and combined with a few walks from this book you have the makings of a superb break. Bishop's Castle hosts several festivals, is a paradise for lovers of real ale and has a great annual walking festival. What more can I say?

1. Start from outside the Castle Hotel in Salop Street, looking downhill, and turn right into the Market Square, a small one at that, and on your left is the fascinating seventeenth century House on Crutches. Continue along Welsh Street, appropriately enough, towards Wales. The chances are that this was one of the key routes leading to the Kerry Ridgeway, a main artery between the two countries in previous centuries. On the right, to the rear of the Castle Hotel are the scant remains of the motte and bailey castle, hence the town's name.

2. Leave the old houses behind and take the first turning on the left to walk through modern housing. Go right at the first junction to cross a stile into a field. Continue to a stile and ahead to another in the next field, climbing gently all of the while away from town. Press on up mid-field at first but then slightly left up the bank by the trees and onto a stile in the top far left-hand corner of the field. There's a good view back across the town.

3. This leads to a road, Kerry Road and part of the Kerry Ridgeway. Go right up to the corner, with an old farm, Caeglas, to the right. Your way is through the gate on the left. At first, keep to the field boundary on the left but as this falls away continue ahead to cross a stile. Continue ahead with a hedge on your right to the next stile. Cross this and walk through a small wood. Go through here to a road.

4. Turn right and drop down to a corner where you bear right through a barred gate to an enclosure. Keep company with the hedge on the left as you begin to climb up to a stile. Cross it and continue uphill as the gradient eases and you see a barred gate ahead. However, go left over a stile before reaching the barred gate. What a view below as this path drops into Colebatch. This is very much sheep farming country and the isolated farms are dotted on the spring line. Descend ahead to the stream below where a way-mark post is a useful guide. Turn left and take a walk in the downstream direction, through two stiles by gates to the road.

5. Now it is time to walk slowly in a very tranquil valley so as to savour it. Continue ahead with your first stile of many to cross in this section. Go through the first very long field to cross a stile ahead. In the next smaller pasture go over a footbridge and follow the field hedge ahead again. Cross a stile into the next field and then ahead through another pasture to cross a further stile. You should come to a point at the end of a longer meadow where you see a gate and stile on your right. Do not go through them. Instead, go left up the hillside passing by the old quarry scar (to your left) to the field corner where you cross the stile.

6. Your return section is straightforward. Simply continue ahead through the fields with the hedge to the right until you reach a track. The track descends to a stile by a gate and then ahead by a number of houses on the outskirts of town. It curves to the right and then left before reaching a lane by the church. Go right and then left into the main street where the Six Bells brewery tap beckons.

4. Bridgnorth

Easy walking, with a few climbs, in the rolling countryside and along a beautiful section of the Mor Brook to the Severn. Other highlights include the Severn Valley Railway and Daniel's Mill. The woodland section near the Mor Brook can get very wet.

Distance	5.5 miles (9km)
Allow	2-3 hours
Map	OS Explorer 218 Wyre Forest and Kidderminster
By train	The Severn Valley railway operates a steam hauled service from Kidderminster on most days of the summer and at weekends and holidays throughout the year
By bus	There are daily bus services from Shrewsbury and Wolverhampton and on Mondays to Saturdays from Ludlow, Kidderminster and Telford
By car	Bridgnorth is on the main A458 between Shrewsbury and Wolverhampton. There are several car parks in town
Refreshments	There are a wide range of cafes, shops and inns in Bridgnorth as well as The Railwayman's Arms at Bridgnorth railway station
Nearest Tourist Information Office	The Library, Listley Street, Bridgnorth Tel: 01746 763257

1. Start from the Tourist Information Centre in Listley Street. Go right from the entrance to walk down Railway Street to the main road and

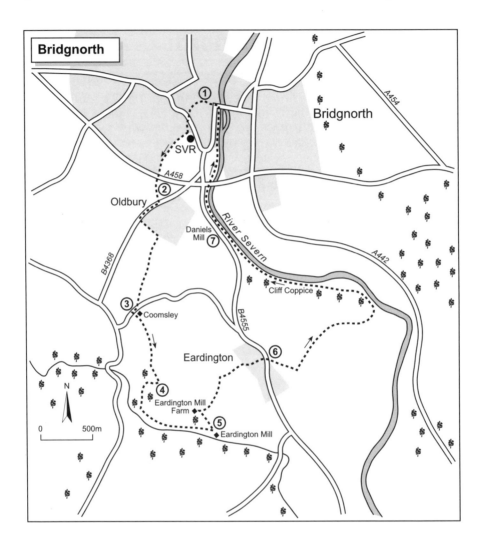

cross over into Station Lane and just as this bends to the right for the Severn Valley Railway overflow car park, go right as signposted up a path which rises to a recreational ground. Your way is ahead across the green to join a perimeter fence and hedge. Cross a stile and walk up a drive to cross a road. Then proceed to the top right corner of the ground where the path bends to the right and over a footbridge across the by-pass road.

2. The path runs along the hedge on the left and then turns right to rise up to the only traditional V-shaped stile I have found remaining in the county. Photograph it and then climb over with ease! Keep left to walk by the church of St Nicholas to a road. Go right and cross over the road by Manor Farm Lane. Just beyond, go left over a stile into a field and walk down to a line of trees where another path comes in from the left. Walk along the line of trees to cross a stile. Now, head slightly left across a field and the path then dips down to a footbridge. Here there is a choice of paths. Go slightly right across the field in the direction of a white house. Cross a stile onto the road.

3. Go right to pass the house and then cross a stile on the left. Go ahead through the meadow and cross a stile. Continue ahead to cross another stile and then pass a cottage where you exit by a fourth stile into a field. There's a farm over to the right. Your way is ahead to cross a stile and then aim slightly right for the wood's edge. Do not enter the wood here but keep ahead to the far corner. Cross a stile.

4. Go right at this point into the wood and the bridleway, which soon bends to the left and runs through woodland to be joined by another coming in from the right. Proceed ahead to go through the gate and soon the wood opens up. Keep ahead and go through another gate. The wood nears the brook; you'll probably hear the babbling waters first and if it is quiet there are often deer in this vicinity. The path narrows and becomes less distinct as it comes closer to the Mor Brook and meanders through wet ground. It then suddenly reaches a green swathe leading up to an old mill converted to a house.

5. You come to a drive and your way is left out of the valley; it is a bit of a climb after miles of easy walking so gear yourself up for it. The road passes by Mill Farm and, just beyond, you need to look for a stile on the right. Cross it and go slightly right through a gap in the hedge. Then, aim slightly right to cross a stile in the next hedge. Proceed slightly left across the next field to a barred gate and onto a road. Go right here for Eardington.

6. At the main road in the village, go right and then next left (as signposted). You have the privilege here of crossing the tracks of the Severn Valley Railway, especially if you can hear the train coming up the valley; make sure you are well clear. Walk through a delightful

wooded section to a track. Go left here and follow this to a gate and stile above a dry valley. Cross the stile and walk down the valley. Before the sewerage works cross a stile and keep left to walk along a perimeter fence of Cliff Coppice. This path joins the Severn Way. Keep ahead on this well way-marked route to Daniel's Bridge where you can gain access to the mill from the way. The mill is the largest waterwheel powered mill remaining in England, It produces, principally, wholemeal flour.

7. In recent years there has been a problem with the collapsing river bank in this area and diversions were in hand at the time of route checking. Needless to say, the path has been re-instated and there's a continuous, rather than diversionary, route into Bridgnorth again. Keep ahead under the by-pass and walk ahead (rather than forking left) between the houses and river. The path finally gives out before the bridge in Low Town. Cross Underhill and either choose to walk up St Mary's Steps and back along Cartway into town, or better still, ride the Cliff Railway (the oldest and steepest funicular in England), back up the 111 feet of the sandstone edge. The choice is yours!

5. Broome

A superb walk along paths and bridleways in what is best described as an engaging landscape. Special features include the Arbor Tree in Aston-on-Clun and the secluded church at Hopesay.

Distance	5 miles (8km)
Allow	2-3 hours
Map	OS Explorer 217 The Long Mynd and Wenlock Edge
By train	There is a daily service from Shrewsbury on the Heart of Wales line to Broome. This is a request stop so you will have to let the conductor guard know that you require Broome and on the return journey have to hold you arm out to signal to the driver that you want the train to stop. All adds to the fun!
By bus	The Secret Hills Shuttle bus runs from Craven Arms, Clun and Bishop's Castle to a stop near to the Kangaroo Inn, Aston-on-Clun. This operates from early April to late September only. There is also a very limited service between Ludlow, Craven Arms and Aston-on-Clun provided by Minsterley Motors on Mondays and Fridays
By car	Broome is on the B4367 between Craven Arms and Hopton Heath. Parking is very limited near to the railway station
Refreshments	The Engine and Tender pub at Broome and The Kangaroo Inn at Aston-on-Clun
Nearest Tourist Information Office	Shropshire Hills Discovery Centre Craven Arms discovery.centre@shropshire.gov.uk

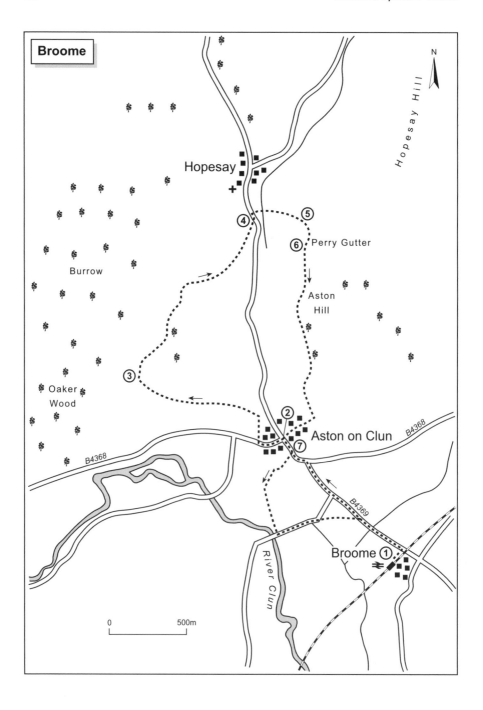

Broome

N

Hopesay Hill

Hopesay

④

⑤

⑥ Perry Gutter

Burrow

Aston
Hill

③

Oaker
Wood

②

B4368

Aston on Clun

⑦

B4368

B4369

Broome ①

River Clun

0   500m

Broome used to be something of a railhead for agricultural goods but is now a single platform; the old goods sheds have been put to other uses. This small village is nestled around the station. Up the road a little is Aston-on-Clun which is a curious place. Not only does it have a pub called The Kangaroo Inn (and there cannot be too many of those about) but it also has two stone built round houses. Even more intriguing is the 'Arbor Tree', which is to this day decorated with flags to commemorate the marriage of local Squire Marston of Oaker to Mary Carter of Sibdon Carwood on Arbor day, 29 May, 1786. It sounds so romantic and to help the annual event into posterity the couple set aside monies for the villagers to festoon the tree on a yearly basis. The old tree fell in 1995 but has since been replaced with another black poplar spliced from the original wood. Ceremonies of a similar nature were commonplace a century earlier when trees were decorated at the command of King Charles II to celebrate the restoration of the monarchy on 29 May, 1660. Very few such ceremonies have survived into the twenty-first century, the most colourful being the garlanding at Castleton in Derbyshire.

1. Start your walk from Broome Railway Station. If you wish to start at Aston then a good place to join is at the Arbor Tree (see point 2). Leave Broome railway station and at the main road in the village go left. Pass by the Engine and Tender public house and continue ahead along this relatively quiet lane to Aston. Turn left to pass by a round house, the garage cum shop and The Kangaroo public house. Cross the road with care and continue ahead to the junction where the Arbor Tree stands. There's information here; a tribute to the pride of the villagers in recent decades.

2. Walk ahead towards Clun passing the Malt House to the left and the hall to your right. Just beyond, turn right along track which actually runs by the hall. At a crossroads go left and this eventually leads to a bridle gate following a wet patch by a small pool.

3. Go right here along a sunken track of some antiquity. Ignore the stile on the left. Simply follow the old lane up the valley, which is easier said than done. This may be a classic country walk rich in wildlife but much of it exists in the track and you may have to make minor deviations at times. Follow it to a bridle gate and upward to a barred gate. The track narrows and you go through another bridle gate to descend towards Hopesay.

4. Go left into Hopesay and left again up to the church, a place of solace in this lovely corner of the village. The church dates from Norman times and has an attractive Norman arched doorway. Nearby are several distinctive houses including the old rectory. Retrace your steps back to the junction at the southern edge of the hamlet where you previously reached the road. Within a matter of fifty metres, go through a traditional iron kissing gate on the left. Walk ahead by the hedge on the left, cross the bridge and head slightly right here up the bank to cross a stile.

5. Look back over Hopesay before going through a kissing gate. It is easy to see now why the settlement grew up in this particular part of the valley, at a meeting of streams and sheltered by Aston, Burrow and Hopesay hills. It is a pretty place whatever the season but the woodland colours are at their best on a frosty Autumn morning when the sun is climbing over Aston into the valley. If you wish to climb Hopesay Hill then head slightly left up a steep path to the seat and viewpoint where you can take a breather and then retrace your steps. Otherwise, go right to descend by a dwelling at Perry Gutter to a stile and road. Evidently, this was a small hamlet in its own right in earlier times but, as with so many places in Shropshire, there has been a significant decline in population during the past century and, in some instances, even earlier.

6. Go right for a few paces on the road and left through a small gate to climb up the bank. Continue ahead through the wood to a stile. Cross it and proceed ahead to a stile beneath trees; the path meanders a little and is grim under foot in places. Rather like life really. Keep ahead again and walk out of the wood. In the pasture walk in the same direction, above the gorse at first then as a green track into the next field. Continue ahead to the barred gate with dwellings nearby. Go right and the road leads into the village, passing by one of the round houses mentioned earlier, back to the decorated tree.

7. Make your way back to Broome but by way of a different route. Walk towards the Kangaroo public house but then turn right into Redwood Drive. This bends left along a track to a water works. Go through the bridle gate and then ahead to a stile. Cross this and keep ahead, near to the banks of the River Clun and over stiles until you reach a bridge. Once on the road, go left and when this begins to bend to the left cross

a stile on the right. Go diagonally across the field to exit on to the road for Broome. Go right here to retrace your steps back to Broome railway station.

6. Chirk and Selattyn

The Ceiriog Valley, Offa's Dyke and the Chirk aqueduct make the walk to Selattyn varied and full of interest. There are several climbs and two miles of quiet road walking. Although the walk begins and ends in Wales it is mainly in Shropshire. A torch is essential for the last section!

Distance	10 miles (16km)
Allow	5-6 hours
Map	OS Explorer 240 Oswestry
By train	There is a daily service from Shrewsbury and Chester
By bus	There's a daily bus service between Wrexham and Chirk
By car	Chirk is on the main A5 road from Shrewsbury. There is on-street car parking near to the railway station
Refreshments	There are cafés and inns in Chirk, Chirk Bank and The Cross Keys at Selattyn, although it is not normally open at lunchtimes with the exception of Sundays
Nearest Tourist Information Office	Heritage Centre, Oswestry Tel: 01691 662753 owbta@oswestry-welshborders.org.uk

Chirk is a small town with a pleasant atmosphere, despite the constant drone of heavy vehicles. The Afon Ceiriog cuts its way deeply here and the Chirk aqueduct and railway viaduct look spectacular across the valley. Nearby is Chirk Castle, a domesticated fortress set in magnificent grounds. Now owned by The National Trust, it is open to the public throughout the summer.

The walk features Offa's Dyke's Dyke Path, one of fifteen national trails, and this is a good area to see the earthworks built on the order of King Offa of Mercia in the 8th century. If you are considering a walking tour this is one of the places to start. Nearby is also the less well known and researched Wat's Dyke which ran from the Dee to Oswestry. Earthworks can be seen near Rhyn and closer to Gobowen and Oswestry. It obviously served a similar purpose to Offa's construction and is said to be older. Perhaps, Offa's men based their work on this earlier dyke.

1. Start the walk from Chirk railway station, which, as mentioned previously, is in Wales! Walk up the steps from either platform. Cross over to walk by the bus shelter and information board. Continue ahead along Station Road with the railway cutting on your right. At the next junction go right. There's a good view of the aqueduct and viaduct from a special viewing area on the other side of the road. Pass by houses but be sure to cross the road here and go right through the barriers along a path which bears left then ahead with a caravan park to the right. Ignore the right-hand turn at a junction but keep left to descend away from the parkland of Chirk Castle. There's a good view here of the old Glyn tramway, which was established in the 1870s to serve the quarries in the Glyn Ceiriog valley and to carry passengers to and from Chirk railway station; it was an early form of transport integration. Unfortunately, demand dwindled in the 1920s and the tramway was closed in the following decade. In more recent years, a trust has been established to re-instate the tramway which would make a wonderful feature in the valley. Cross over the road and go right down to the bridge. Turn left to walk over the bridge, which spans the beautiful Afon Ceiriog, and you step into Shropshire. Turn first right, as way-marked Maelor Way, into a lane.

2. Just after the telephone kiosk keep ahead to cross a stile by a gate. This is way-marked as part of the Ceiriog Way, walk through the pasture and in the next field alongside the river. The earth works here look very much as if there was a mill or fish pool on this site. Follow the riverside to a stile leading into the woodland owned by the Woodland Trust. This path continues ahead, rising up steps, until it eventually exits by way of a stile into a meadow. Keep slightly left and cross the next stile to join a track. Walk up the lane to the road.

3. Go right and the road bends left and leaves the hamlet of Bronygarth. Look for a track on the left, way-marked as Ceiriog Way. It climbs to a junction where you go right onto another track. There are great views of Chirk castle from this track. This property contains a number of

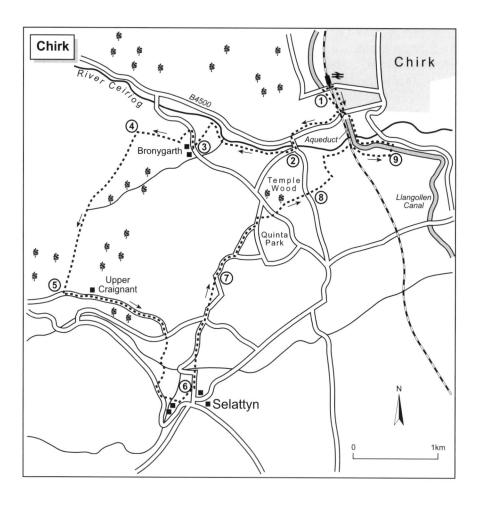

fine state rooms full of Adam style furniture and other artifacts from the past three centuries.

4. After about half a mile you come to Offa's Dyke Path. Walking the Dyke is always interesting as it allows you to exercise your imagination. Why was it built in the first place? Some sections look very much like a defensive earthwork and in others as if it were merely a prominent boundary to mark territory rather than for military purposes. The latter explanation tends to be favoured by historians and it was, no doubt, used to regulate trade between Mercia and Wales. Leave that

one with you to think over. Go left over the stile and follow the dyke along a very clear section until you come to a tarmac lane which you cross. Take care on the next bit as it drops very steeply into a ravine and there's an even steeper climb out of it. Keep ahead on the dyke until you reach another lane which you cross with Mount Wood to your left.

5. On reaching the next lane go left and follow this past Upper Craignant. This road soon descends and bends to the right near to Top Fron. Ignore the turning to the left and the other to the right. Your way is ahead along a 'No Through Road' to the farm. Before the entrance, go right on the old by-way down the hillside, avoiding tracks off to the left or right until you come down to join a larger track and a house by the stream. Go right here for Pant-y-ffynon and climb up another bridleway to a road. Go left and at the corner, with a dwelling to your left, cross a stile by a gate. Follow the hedge down the field to the footbridge over the stream. Notice the stone bridge. Climb up by Selattyn church and the Cross Keys public house which is in the CAMRA National Inventory but unfortunately it is not open at lunchtimes in the week.

   This old village is thought to have been a frontier trading post in the more turbulent past centuries. There are certainly a large number of tracks leading into Selattyn and it is very much a crossroads to this day. The church is at the very centre of the village. Legend has it that an early nobleman found a white hind on this site which led him to dedicate the land for religious purposes. Accordingly, he had an ancient church of Bryn Hen Eglwys removed to here. It has been cherished throughout the centuries and the interior was beautifully restored during Victorian times.

6. Go left, before the pub (a No Through road) and by the church to walk along a lane to a stile into a meadow. Cross it and follow the hedge on your right around to a stile on the right. Take care as this drops down to a lane where you turn left. Follow this down to a bridge; just before go right along a bridleway which crosses the stream and rises up to the road again. Continue ahead at the cross roads and as this lane begins to curve right, go left over a stile and then head slightly right across a large field. You come to another stile in the corner, more or less diagonally ahead. Exit by way of a sleeper bridge onto the lane once again.

7. Go left here to walk down a lane of some antiquity. Keep right at the next junction, left at the next one by Dinas Cottage and right at the next. You will see Quinta Park with the elaborate Victorian house, as the road comes to a fork. Go right beneath the bridge and at the next junction you cross the stile ahead with some relief, no doubt, into parkland. You will see a folly looking like a miniature Stonehenge to your right, one of many pieces of fine stonework throughout the parkland. Go directly ahead and cross the stile leading into the woodland. Ahead is an early pedestrian tunnel which you can avoid if you wish as you continue to the woods edge but please feel free to explore the tunnel to test your torch for the real thing later in the walk. Go ahead down the field to a barred gate by an electric telegraph pole.

8. Once on the road go left, and after 20 metres, turn right through a pedestrian tunnel and up to a stile. Cross it and keep ahead with the hedge to the left. Come to a duet of stiles and once over, aim for the left of the farm buildings where you will find a stile beneath an ivy-clad oak. Cross the stile and go left along the lane. Beyond a house the lane begins to drop into the valley and you go right along a track which climbs up through the woods to a stile. Cross this and go left to the railway. Cross the tracks with care and follow the field's edge to your left. At the last telegraph pole the path cuts off right to another pair of stiles which you cross and then go down to the kissing gate, into Chirk Bank.

9. Go left, cross the canal bridge and go left again along the tow-path. This leads to the magnificent aqueduct engineered by Thomas Telford and there are great views from here. At the other end is your chance to use your torch, for the tow-path leads through the Chirk tunnel to a cutting by the railway, where you turn right and climb up the bank to the station. If you do not fancy this last exciting twist to the walk, then go right up the embankment before the tunnel and cross the road to retrace your steps to the starting point. This option is not nearly so much fun.

7. Church Stretton and Cardington

This is a longer ramble on paths and tracks which involves one strenuous climb. The highlight has to be Caer Caradoc with superb views across the county.

Distance	10 miles (16km)
Allow	5-6 hours
Map	OS Explorer 217 Long Mynd and Wenlock Edge
By train	There is a daily service from Shrewsbury, Ludlow and beyond
By bus	There is an hourly service on Mondays to Saturdays from Ludlow and Shrewsbury which calls into Beaumont Road in Church Stretton and the Shropshire Hills Shuttles also leave from here
By car	Church Stretton is on the A49 between Shrewsbury and Ludlow. There is a car park off Sandford Avenue
Refreshments	There are a number of inns, cafés and shops in Church Stretton. There is also The Royal Oak at Cardington, a long standing Good Beer Guide entry and deservedly so
Nearest Tourist Information Office	Church Stretton TIC Tel: 01694 723133

Not only do the characteristic edges of Caradoc and Lawley bring a sense of awe but the surrounding hills of Hope Bowdler, Helmeth and Willstone have an equal fascination.

Of the walking areas in Shropshire this must be an all-time favourite; the people of the area have signed up too, for Church Stretton is a Walkers are Welcome town. Wherever you wander you'll see the good work. It makes it a good place to stay for the walker. Church Stretton is an engaging little town, which retains its spa influence as well as being a market place for the locality. In fact, it became something of a resort in the last century, and mineral water is still bottled from nearby Cwm Dale. In its heyday, however, at least one historian has pointed to the fact that water was brought up from Llandrindod Wells by train! It is an attractive centre with a mix of accommodation and other facilities, such as The Shuttles, which make it ideal for a few days stay. More importantly, the air always feels just right for walking here.

1. Start at the railway station. Leave from the 'Shrewsbury trains' platform, and walk up the access road to Sandford Avenue. Go right to walk over the railway bridge to the traffic lights on the A49. Cross the main road and walk ahead. Be even more vigilant as you cross the B4371 road to enter Watling Street North.

2. Follow this lane, the old Roman Road, but bear right before a new housing complex, on a 'No Through Road', and you will see an old sunken lane at the top on the right. Keep ahead to the gate and grid but here you cross a stile and walk along the field boundary adjacent to the old road which runs parallel on your right. Follow this to the gateway in the upper corner of the field and walk up the muddy track. Keep to this track at first, after 150-200 metres cross a stream on the left by a footbridge and then the well-worn path which climbs up to a more prominent track. Follow this up the hillside until it bends right. You go left over a prominent stile between hawthorn and hazel on the left. A well-worn path leads up to Caradoc, a very steep climb which will set the heart pacing. You reach a false summit where you'll see the ramparts of the fort.

3. Here are the remains of an Iron Age hill fort standing on Shropshire's most impressive ridge. It is no surprise that this site is also thought to have been Caracticus's last battle with the Romans. With the Roman Road lying below in the valley and the hill fort being such a dramatic site you could well imagine it. By all means walk up to the summit for the views, including an excellent one of Cardington church and village to your right. However, your way is to take the green path which descends to the right before the main outcrop. There's a good view of the Lawley ahead and the ridge known as the Wilderness to the right in the foreground. Cross a stile then proceed across a field, level at

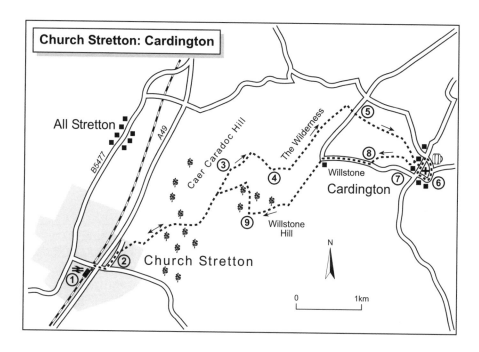

first then a sharp dip down the bank to climb a stile by a barred gate and a track where you go left.

4. The track descends a little and then climbs gently. Ignore the first stile on the left but go for the second stile by a gate on the left. Walk along a ridge, well a gentle sort of ridge, known as the Wilderness. Firstly, head slightly right. Cross a stile by a barred gate and proceed ahead. You pass through old workings and cross another stile. Keep ahead, i.e. ignore the stile on the right and you soon reach a stile by a gate. Follow the track down to a gate and stile onto a road.

5. Cross the road and the stile before you. Follow the hedge to the right until the next stile then after a short distance the path crosses a stile and now runs ahead again with the hedge to your left. Cross two further stiles ahead and, as you come closer to Cardington village, go through a stile or bridle gate at the bottom right corner of a tapered field and continue with a hedge to your left. This leads to a track which takes you the edge of the village where you go through a gate and ahead on a lane between dwellings.

6. The church is ahead at the heart of the village. Turn left and then right and right again for the Royal Oak. The village is a fine collection of traditional stone and half-timbered buildings huddled together around the church. The latter dates partly from Norman times and has a number of interesting aspects including a splendid effigy of Judge William Leighton, one time resident in nearby Plaish Hall. Legend has it that the elaborate chimneys were built by a condemned convict in the hope of receiving a pardon. He hanged nevertheless, some say from the very same chimneys, which doesn't say much for the kindly old judge does it. From the Royal Oak, go right and right again then next left to retrace your way back to the edge of the village.

7. Turn left immediately before reaching the barred gate. The track bends right to the fields, passing by a small plantation. Head slightly left to cross the stile and go right up a narrow field strip, heading for the far left corner. Just before, look for a stile on the left. Cross it and go right keeping the hedge to your right. Cross the next stile and go left. Come to two stiles guarding a footbridge and, once over, head slightly left up the field to another stile. Go slightly left up the field to a stile which leads onto the road.

8. Go right along the road to pass by Willstone Farm. At the junction, go left and then left again over a stile by a barred gate. Go ahead, mid-field, and along a tractor track passing through a gateway with Willstone Hill, and the Battle Stones, towering above you. The track ahead leads to a double barred gate but beforehand go left by wire fencing along a less well-defined path to pass a pool. Cross a stile into rough pasture. Go diagonally across a field to a bridle gate leading into bracken. Continue ahead on the track, keeping parallel to the hedge on the right. Cross a stile and continue ahead through bracken. You reach a meeting of paths by a bridle gate.

9. Keep right here to follow the green way up to a track where you go left. This descends to the stream and woodland encountered on the outward leg of the walk and back to the large field and sunken lane. From here retrace your steps into Church Stretton. This has to be one of Shropshire's classic walks.

8. Church Stretton: The Long Mynd

This ramble has several climbs but each one offering marvellous views. The walk is mainly on paths. The highlight is the climb up Ashes Hollow to The Long Mynd and the descent into Carding Mill Valley. Be prepared to get your feet wet crossing the brook as it tumbles down Ashes Hollow.

Distance	8 miles (13km)
Allow	4 hours
Map	OS Explorer 217 Church Stretton
By train	There is a daily service from Shrewsbury, Ludlow and beyond
By bus	There is an hourly service on Mondays to Saturdays from Ludlow and Shrewsbury which calls into Beaumont Road in Church Stretton and the Shropshire Hills Shuttles also leave from here. For those who want an easier option catch the Shuttles bus to the Shooting Box and walk back down from point 6
By car	Church Stretton is on the A49 between Shrewsbury and Ludlow. There is a car park off Sandford Avenue
Refreshments	There are a number of inns, cafés and shops in Church Stretton. There's also The Ragleth and The Green Dragon public houses at Little Stretton. In addition, the National Trust Chalet Pavilion, which is heated by an amazing wood burner, is a great place to gather information and take tea. Wood is sourced from their nearby Wenlock Edge estate with an estimated saving of carbon dioxide emissions of 10 tons per year
Nearest Tourist Information Office	Church Stretton TIC Tel: 01694 723133

The Long Mynd is a high plateau disturbed only by narrow ravines known locally as 'batches', cutting their way eastwards. These were formed at the latter stages of the last ice age when the ice sheets and glaciers were melting. The Mynd itself comprises mud and sands deposited in the seas of million of years ago. It is carpeted in heather, bracken and bilberry and as such is ideal for grouse. There are also a number of birds seen in Shropshire upland hills such as the kestrel, wheatear and sometimes the raven, especially in Ashes Hollow where they have re-colonised since the 1980s. If you want to know more then the Smith, Uff and Carty book, *Wild Mynd*, is a good enough companion. It is great walking territory and despite its popularity on Bank Holidays and warm Sundays it is still quiet at other times. It is very much a place to uplift the spirits.

1. Start at Church Stretton railway station. Leave the station from the platform where trains depart in the Shrewsbury direction. Follow the access road to Sandford Avenue and turn left into this main shopping street. This leads up to a cross roads where you go left into the Square (there's a small farmer's market here on the second and fourth Friday of the month). Go right at the end of the Square along Churchway to pass the parish church to Rectory Woods and Field, a superb success for the town in its approach to enhancing nearby biodiversity with access to woodland and the wildness of The Mynd beyond.

2. Go ahead in the field on a well worn path to the wood, which you enter through a kissing gate. Go right to climb up to a footbridge at a place known as Yew Tree Retreat where there's a pool. Follow the stream, Town Brook, to a kissing gate at the wood's edge and old reservoir.

3. Turn left here and the path soon curves right to rise steeply; it is a boundary between wood and wilderness. Take breath as you reach a stile. Go over this and now descend The Hundred Steps to pass by a bungalow to Cunnery Road. Go right here and there's a trail to the left to the Long Mynd Hotel but your way is on a well worn track which descends to Crossbanks. The paths in this area have been championed and re-opened to their former glory in recent years by the Shropshire Ramblers Association (and others). Their good work makes this walk, and other circular strolls, possible.

4. On reaching the road, go right and right again up a path which runs between gardens and skirts Hope's Wood, a Site of Special Scientific

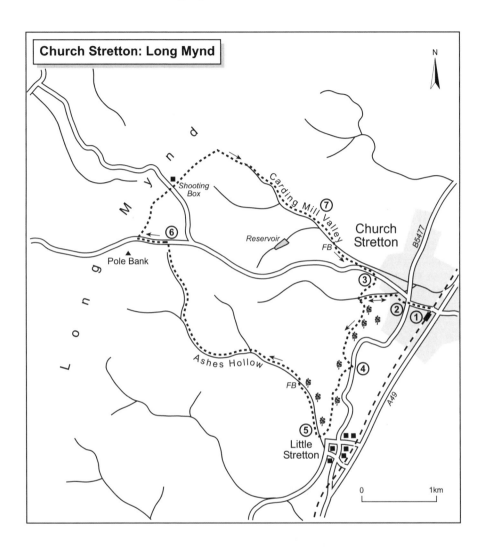

Interest. Cross the stile and climb slightly left up the hillside up to cross another stile into a large pasture. Continue at first alongside the fence but then ease away as the path bends towards a barn and the far left corner. Cross a stile by the right of a barn and now keep ahead along a narrow path among the oak trees which survive on this scree slope. You'll need neat footwork to survive too so concentrate. The path descends into the valley and down to a stile to exit onto the road.

5. Go right over the footbridge across the bubbling waters of the Ash Brook. Once over, turn right over to cross a stile to enter a camping field so you'll have to make your way between the tents. Proceed ahead to another stile and progress ahead on the clear path. Cross another stile and a footbridge over the stream to pass by cottages. The path now keeps close to the banks of the Ash Brook as it cuts its way down the batch. It crosses from side to side up to a confluence of streams so you might get wet after rain. At this point the path keeps right and then left to climb up steps to rise away from the waterside on the hillside. It then bends left to run along the hillside above the stream. The path eventually meets with the stream again. Make your way up to the heather heath and to the road.

6. Go left at the road and in 20 metres bear right on a track (the Pole Bank Walk). This climbs to a junction where you meet the Shropshire Way. Go right and the track reaches the Shooting Box where you cross the road and passes by a car park. The track soon joins another where you

The Long Mynd above Church Stretton

keep left and continue ahead until you reach the next junction of tracks. Your route is way-marked as Carding Mill Valley. Go right at the junction and right again within metres to descend into the valley. The view across to Ragleth and Helmeth hills is spectacular. The bridle-path, known as Mott's Road at this point, drops more steeply into the valley. At the junction of paths do not go left to Light Spout Hollow but continue ahead over the tributary stream to reach the upper car park.

7. Descend the valley, beyond the turning circle for cars and alongside the brook, known as Mott's Road, squeezing between Calf Ridge and Haddon Hill. Beyond the Chalet Pavilion tea room and shop and before the stream passes beneath the road, bear right along a path which rises up the hillside to the Burway (there's a cattle grid and gate here). Cross the road and walk ahead until you reach the gate where you exited from Rectory Wood on the outward section. Go left here to retrace your steps to Church Stretton which rightly proclaims its Walkers are Welcome initiative.

9. Cleobury Mortimer

A very rewarding walk through undulating dairy country. Mainly on footpaths with a few road sections. Few harsh climbs.

Distance	7 miles (11km)
Allow	4 hours
Map	OS Explorer 203 Ludlow, Tenbury Wells and Cleobury Mortimer
By bus	There is a daily bus service, 292, between Ludlow and Kidderminster (Birmingham)
By car	Travel on the A4117 between Ludlow and Bewdley. Park in the centre of Cleobury Mortimer
Refreshments	There are cafés, shops and inns at Cleobury Mortimer
Nearest Tourist Information Office	Castle St, Ludlow Tel: 01584 875053 info@ludlow.org.uk

Cleobury Mortimer is a small town well known for its church with a crooked spire. The 1828 Business Directory produced by Tibnance and Company of Shrewsbury described it as 'not a place of much trade' but it seems to have survived into the 21st century.

Cleobury (pronounced 'Clibbery') was mentioned in the Domesday Book and has always been a thoroughfare across the River Rea. Its main street has a handsome collection of Georgian Town houses and there are also several traditional shop fronts leading out onto the road. The church, however, is a central feature and has a plaque and a stained glass window to commemorate William Langland, born in 1330, and author of *The Vision of Piers Plowman.* Cleobury and Ledbury, (in Herefordshire) both claim to have been the birthplace of this contemporary of Chaucer! In more recent times Cleobury Mortimer has been the home to a local postman poet, Simon Evans and a road has now been named after him.

The footpath network has been improved considerably in recent years thanks to the work of the Cleobury Mortimer Footpath Association. Take a look at their website (just google the name) and you will find several local walks which can be downloaded. It is an ideal location for a weekend away in a less well known part of the county.

1. Start the ramble from Talbot Inn, turn right along High Street towards Ludlow and at the first cross roads go left into the Tenbury Wells road just before the garage. This curves right by new housing and as you climb away from the village go left into a drive by a veterinary surgeons. Keep to the right and walk up to a stile by a barred gate. You can see Hobson's Brewery to the left.

2. Head slightly right, keeping to the left of the electric telegraph poles, and soon you will see a track between pools to cross a stile. This can get a bit messy at times so tread carefully. Go over the stile on the right towards the top of the field. Cross this next large field in a slightly left direction towards the impressive oak, some way to the left of the cottage. Go over a stile here and a road; then proceed over two more stiles ahead. The path is clear enough. Go left after the second stile to cross another stile into the next field. Once over turn right to walk along a fence.

3. Cross the road and a stile, with Barnslands Farm down the track to your left. Descend the field, heading slightly left, where you will find a stile situated to the right of a corrugated barn and cross another. Now, head slightly right to join a hedge on the right and follow this down to a sunken track on the left, as it curves left, in a peaceful valley beneath Dirtybridge Covert. The track bends right where you cross the stile by a barred gate now climbing up a bank towards a small disused building. Go left before the buildings, again crossing a stile adjacent to a gate. You bear slightly right heading for a point where the fence on the left meets the wood.

4. Cross the stile beneath the hazel bush and the path plunges fairly dramatically down to the stream but with steps to help the descent. Cross the footbridge and climb up to the stile. Head down towards the River Rea, a sleepy little river not well known, but which is beautifully fresh and full of wildlife. Continue near to the river banks to cross the stile and through woodland and soon you will see the old railway line.

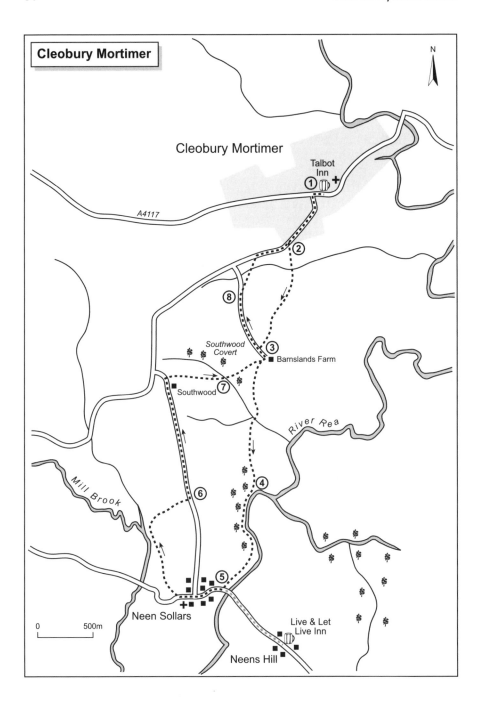

Cleobury Mortimer

N

Talbot Inn

A4117

Southwood Covert

Barnslands Farm

Southwood

River Rea

Mill Brook

Neen Sollars

Live & Let Live Inn

Neens Hill

0   500m

What a splendid line this one must have been. There's a choice of two stiles here. Keep ahead, however, across the footbridge and climb up the railway embankment. Go right and after about 100 metres go left to cross a stile. Then keep right and the path becomes more overgrown, winding its way through bracken and descending to the river once again through stinking hellebore and the like. People walk here but it is overgrown in summer. This area can be subject to flooding too! Cross another stile and proceed ahead to a road. This is Neen Sollars, a small hamlet which once had its own station on the Bewdley to Tenbury Wells and Woofferton Junction railway. It is a sleepy little place with an appealing church but the Railway public house has long since gone. However, if you are walking of a summer's eve or at the weekend you can make a half mile diversion to climb up to Neens Hill where the Live and Let Live public house welcomes walkers.

5. Otherwise, go right here by the bridge and walk through Neen Sollars, keep ahead at the junction and continue by what was the Railway pub (now Tavern House) and the church. As the road curves left, go right over a stile by a gate adjacent to a restored house. Continue uphill, well to the right of the farm, and head towards the right-hand hedge where you cross a stile. People keep horses here so it might well be fenced.

    Once over the stile, go slightly left through an orchard to a gateway. Cross the stile in the dip and walk ahead to follow the track along the wood to a fishing pool. Keep to the right bank and go ahead to a stile by a gate into the field. Climb up the bank, heading slightly left and eventually levelling out to a barred gate. Go through this and keep ahead to a stile leading to a lane.

6. Go left and stroll along this quiet lane for well over half a mile to reach Southwood Farm. As the road bears left you go right, as signed, into the field and to the left of the farmyard to the gate. Bear slightly right across the field to skirt the farm, and then go ahead to cross a stile by a barred gate. Head slightly left down the bank to a footbridge over the stream to the left of a remnant piece of hedge. Go over the bridge and through the gate.

7. The path climbs up, slightly right and steeply through Southwood Covert. It is a bit of a climb up to a stile by a gate into the field. Once over, head almost directly ahead up the bank to a stile, which can be

seen on the horizon. Go through it and keep ahead again to a stile which leads onto a track. Go left through a gateway to the track. Ignore the junction to the right near the house.

8. As the track descends look for a stile on the right into a field. Head slightly left across the field to cross a footbridge and proceed in a similar direction in the next field to the far right corner. You exit onto the road and then go right for the return road section into Cleobury Mortimer. Let the crooked spire guide you.

10. Clun

Easy to moderate walk with one long climb to Bury Ditches. It is a must for those who like to get away from it all. The highlight of the walk is Bury Ditches and dropping down into the villages of Clun and Clunton.

Distance	6 miles (10km)
Allow	3 hours
Map	OS Explorer 201 Knighton and Presteigne; 216 Welshpool and Montgomery
By bus	There is a very limited bus service from Ludlow and Craven Arms on Mondays and Fridays. The best way to travel is on the Shropshire Hills Shuttles from Craven Arms or Bishop's Castle to Clun on Saturdays, Sundays and Bank Holidays which operates from early April to the end of September
By car	Follow the B4368 from Craven Arms through to Clun. There is a car park in the village
Refreshments	The White Horse or Sun Inn, Clun or the Crown Inn at Clunton. There are cafes and shops in Clun
Nearest Tourist Information Office	Shropshire Hills Discovery Centre, Craven Arms Tel: 03456 789024 discovery.centre@shropshire.gov.uk

Clun is a divided community. To the north of the river, nestled around the dramatic ruins of the castle, is the Norman township and to the south of the ancient Clun Bridge is a much older settlement bordering the large church which has overlooked the village for centuries. The castle is an attraction in its own right as is the local town trail. People love to sit by

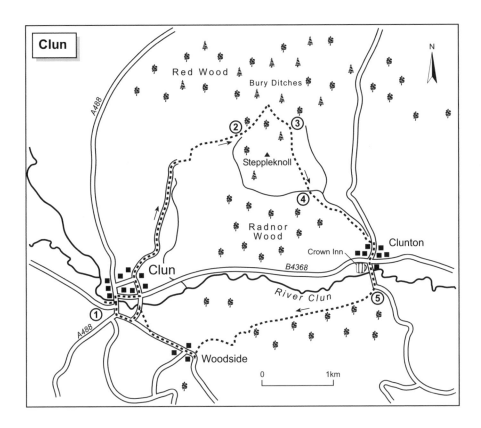

the river and watch the ducks going about their daily business. This is one of Houseman's quietest parts as is Clunton, to be found mid way on the walk. You would not think so if you turn up to the Green Man Festival in Spring or the valley beer fest later in the year; the village lets it hair down on these occasions.

1. Start the walk from the bus stop at the car park by the old packhorse bridge. Go over the bridge and walk up to High Street. Go right at the junction and turn left into Ford Street; Clun youth hostel is signposted this way. At the end of Ford Street turn right, pass the youth hostel and follow the lane for about a mile as it rises to the old farmstead of Guilden Down. Keep right at the junction here and continue ahead, keeping left as you pass a dwelling on the way up to Bury Ditches,

thought to be one of the finest Iron Age Hillforts in the UK. It is difficult, however, to discern the shape of the fort from this walk.

2. Enter the wood and rise up ahead to join a main track. Continue ahead to reach a summit where the Shropshire Way bears left. However, follow the John Mytton Way on a forestry track ahead to the corner where it bends to the right. Go right here along a footpath through denser woodland and down the hillside. You will come to a fork. Keep right here to rise up to the next junction where you turn left. The hillfort lies across the valley beneath tree cover.

3. The track begins to bend to the right. Look for a stile here on the left. Go over this and turn right to follow the perimeter fence and then drop down to the stile by a barred gate onto a track. Walk ahead up to a barred gate and stile. Once through, keep ahead towards the farm but bear left by the barn to go through another barred gate. The track runs ahead but your way is to the right through a barred gate into a pasture. This track descends to a barred gate where you cross a stream and through another gate.

The medieval bridge at Clun

4. Bear left in this next pasture to walk away from the stream a little, to cross a stile. Walk ahead in the next large grazing pasture. Cross a stile located by a barred gate nearer to the slope than the stream. Cross this stile and now walk closer to the stream. Go through a gate on the left. Cross a stile by the stream and go left alongside the stream. Go through the stile by a gate and head slightly left where you go over the stile onto the road. Go right to the crossroads in the village of Clunton; the Crown Inn stands just to the right and it would be a pity not to call in. Your way is directly across onto a lane which crosses the River Clun and then, not far beyond, to a cottage at a corner.

5. Go right here through a gate and rise on a wonderful woodland track through Sowdley Wood. This runs more or less ahead for the best part of a mile then curves its way to exit into farmland. Meet a track coming in from the left and keep ahead to the road. Go right and follow this past a farm. As the road descends look for a stile on the right. Cross it and walk slightly left to a stile which exits onto a road.

6. Go left here and climb up the hill to pass by the church. Then turn right to descend to the ancient packhorse bridge where the walk began.

11. Cound

Easy walking through the valley of the Coundmoor Brook. The highlights are the tranquillity of the woodland, the views across the Cound Hall and Cound church. There's a small section of main road to The Riverside Inn but otherwise mainly uses footpaths.

Distance	5 miles (8km)
Allow	2½ hours
Map	OS Explorer 241 Shrewsbury
By bus	The 436/7 bus runs at regular intervals, daily, between Shrewsbury and Bridgnorth. Ask for the turning to Cound Fishery
By car	Cound is on the A458 road between Shrewsbury and Much Wenlock. There is limited parking beyond the junction
Refreshments	The Riverside Inn at Cound is open all day in the summer months
Nearest Tourist Information Office	Rowley's House, Barker Street Tel: 01743 281200

The small village of Cound has a history inextricably linked to the River Severn for it once had a port here for trans-shipment of coal and other goods. The railway to Buildwas Junction (the Severn Valley line) also served the village. However, on the other side of the road is the older settlement nestled around the parish church which dates from the 13th century.

1. Start from the turning to Cound and Kenley. Walk down the road ahead to a bridge over the Cound Brook. Just beforehand, go right through a barred gate and then head slightly left across pasture to a footbridge. Go over this and walk up to a path between gardens. This gives out onto a road in Upper Cound.

2. Go left and walk ahead at the next junction. Leave the hamlet and as the road bends right, keep ahead along a track to enter a field. There's a great view of the Wrekin from here. The path heads slightly right across the field down to a footbridge over the Coundmoor Brook. Go over and turn right. Cross another stile and keep ahead to another. Simply follow the stream up to the wood where there's a stile by a gate. Cross this and proceed through a wood replete with bluebells in Spring and with the smell of wild garlic in the air.

3. You'll reach a wet patch just before a junction. Go right here to cross the footbridge. The track passes by pools on the left. The forest track bends right and you will see a waymark post under the shade of a large conifer. Your way is slightly left to a barred gate to enter the meadow. Follow the path ahead to the gate leading onto the road.

4. Go left to cross the bridge by the ford and walk up the bank past a cottage and junction. Just a little beyond go left through a barred gate. The bridleway crosses a stream. Keep right and walk by the hedge up to a gate and into the wood. The bridleway reaches a dwelling and just

The church at Cound

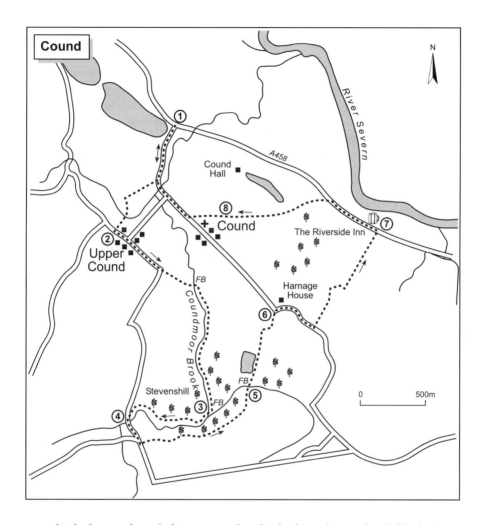

a little beyond go left on a path which dips down the hillside to a kissing gate.

5. Head slightly right across the field to another kissing gate which you go through. You will see a pool to the right. Go over a footbridge and the path leads left and rises up the wooded slope to a kissing gate and a pasture. Skirt around the right hand rim of a pool. If you look carefully on the map it shows the right of way going through the pool. I'd stick to the dry land on this occasion. Cross a stile and keep ahead

The Wrekin is a landmark on this walk

to a hedge leading to a corner where you go over another stile on the right. Proceed ahead to a track where you go left to reach a road.

6. This is the quiet hamlet of Harnage. Turn right by Harnage House and walk up to a point where the road bends right and a way is signposted left down a drive towards a cottage. As you approach the double gates next to it, you'll see a gap to the right of them. Go through here and the path bends to the right. At the junction, go left to leave the farm buildings behind. Follow the track down the field; there's a great view of the Wrekin. As the track bends left you go right. On reaching the stile in the hedge, go left over it and walk down the field to a dwelling. The path runs to the left of the house and then follows the field's edge down to the main road.

7. There follows a short road section which requires more care and attention as the traffic is moving faster. Cross the road and walk facing the traffic. The Riverside Inn (which used to be Cound's railway station) is on the right so it might be time for refreshment! Otherwise, continue ahead past a showroom and on the verge until you reach an

entrance to a house on the left. Cross the road again and walk a few paces down the entrance road. Here you go right into a field and head slightly left with the house and garden to your left. Go through the small gate and over the drive and then through another small gate. Proceed ahead through a large field. The path runs parallel to a field edge and then bends slightly left towards the church. You will catch a glimpse of Cound Hall, a magnificent red brick building dating from the early 18th century.

8. Cross a stile and then proceed to go through a kissing gate. Head slightly right to skirt the old dovecote and walk into the churchyard to pass by the parish church, dating from the 13th century but with many additions from the 19th century. The gargoyles can be clearly seen as you leave to join a road; keep a look out for them. Go right and right again at the next junction to return to the starting point.

12. Craven Arms

A moderately strenuous walk with some climbs. The highlight of the walk is Wenlock Edge and there are great views from Callow Hill if you choose to detour to Flounder's Folly — a strenuous climb.

Distance	6 miles (10km)
Allow	3 hours
Map	OS Explorer 217 The Long Mynd and Wenlock Edge
By train	There is a regular daily service between Shrewsbury and Ludlow stopping at Craven Arms in addition to the Heart of Wales line trains. It is a ten minutes walk from the railway station through town to the Discovery Centre. From the station entrance go right down a narrow path behind houses, Tuffins supermarket and arrive at the Craven Arms Hotel
By bus	There is a regular bus 435 on Mondays to Saturdays from Shrewsbury and Ludlow
By car	Craven Arms is situated on the A49 road between Shrewsbury and Ludlow. There is car parking in the town centre
Refreshments	There are several inns, cafés and shops in Craven Arms as well as a café and shop at the Shropshire Hills Discovery Centre
Nearest Tourist Information Office	Shropshire Hills Discovery Centre, Craven Arms Tel: 03456 789024 discovery.centre@shropshire.gov.uk

Craven Arms was once a major railway junction, with not only trains bound for the Heart of Wales line (then known as The Central Wales line), but also to Buildwas Junction and in earlier times also to Bishop's Castle.

It also had a thriving market and thousands of sheep were transported to the town by train in its heyday. At the edge of the town is the Shropshire Hills Discovery Centre, a great place for information. You can visit the Shropshire Hills Exhibition, or go for local walks in the Onny Meadows, so put it on the list of places to see. The shuttles for the Clun Valley leave from here too. A half mile beyond the Onny Meadows lies Stokesay Castle which is linked by The Shropshire Way. This fortified manor dating from the 13th century is managed by English Heritage.

1. Start the walk from the Discovery Centre. Leave from the rear of the building to walk in the direction of the Onny Meadows. Go left at the first junction to pass the Community Garden. Walk ahead on a road which narrows to a footbridge over the River Onny.

2. There's a choice of paths here. Keep ahead (just to the right of the electric telegraph pole). As you approach the next boundary cross a stile; ignore the bridge to the right. Now, keep ahead with the hedge and stream to your right. This leads up to the top left field corner. Cross a stile and the road with care. Go over a stile to enter a large field. Walk ahead with the hedge to your right. Climb a stile beneath a large oak tree and proceed ahead again up to another stile. The climbing begins as you rise up through Halford Wood to a stile near

Walking to Dinchope

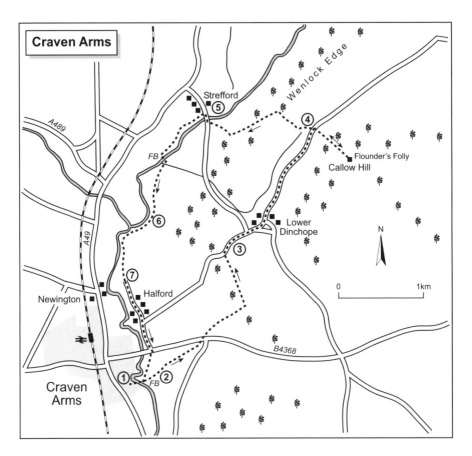

the summit. There's a way-mark post to guide you. Bear left on the grassy bluff and there are good views to be had along here. The path, however, soon moves away from the top. Aim for the far right corner of the pasture where there is a gate leading on to the road. Go right.

3 Keep ahead at both junctions to walk into the hamlet of Lower Dinchope. At the third junction go left and follow this for a good half a mile to where it bends left and a forestry track runs to the right. You may well have seen Flounder's Folly on the top of Callow Hill when you climbed up. Commissioned by Benjamin Flounders in 1838, seemingly to employ locals at a time of depression or simply to show his commitment to his Shropshire Estate, this wealthy businessman left a tower which offers magnificent views across the county. It is possible

Flounder's Folly

to make the detour here for the walk up to the tower. Follow the track up to a junction where a bridleway (Ride UK) peels off left. Continue upwards and the track bends to the right to the tower. Retrace your steps after catching your breath.

4. Otherwise, back at the corner, you need to walk down the bank to a triangle where you go left again and as the road bends right go ahead up a track to Wenlock Edge into Strefford Wood. Turn left and when you come to the first junction go right down the hillside. Follow this track down to a crossroads of tracks and a pool of standing water. Keep ahead here down a sunken lane which exits the woodland. On reaching the road go left and then right to cross the ford.

5. Keep ahead at Strefford if you are going to visit the Strefford Hall Farm Shop (closed Mondays). Otherwise, turn left at the next junction to walk through the hamlet. Leave by way of a bridle gate into a field and walk to the corner where you keep ahead to another bridle gate. Keep ahead near to the Quinny Brook. Cross a stile and keep ahead with the stream to your left. Cross the footbridge over the brook and keep ahead for about 30 metres before turning right to cross a much smaller footbridge. Keep ahead to cross a stile and ahead in the same direction through two more fields to join a track ahead to pass by houses and outbuildings.

6. Cross a stile by a barred gate into the next field and head slightly right between woods and then bend left to reach a bridle gate leading into a wood. Cross a double stile and keep ahead and through a barred gate. Proceed ahead again to pass two magnificent trees towards Newington. Go in the same direction but keeping to the right of a remnant of a hedge and onward to the edge of the field to cross a stile on the right. Cross it and walk ahead along a corralled path which leads by a dwelling to Halford Lane.

7. Follow this through to the B4368. Turn right and, if you are heading from the railway station, it is best to walk along here into town and to the path at the rear of the Tuffins car park, where you go right. If you are returning to the Discovery Centre, then cross the road before the bridge over the river and cross a stile to follow a well worn path through the pasture. This follows the river and then bends right to the bridge over the River Onny where you began your walk.

13. Ellesmere

Easy walking along tracks and the Shropshire Union Canal (Llangollen Branch) tow-path.

Distance	11 miles (17-18km)
Allow	4-5 hours
Map	OS Explorer 241 Shrewsbury
By bus	There is a limited bus service from Oswestry to Welshampton. It is far more frequent to Ellesmere. There is a regular daily service to Ellesmere from Shrewsbury. They all call at Cross Street where it is a few minutes walk to the Square and Wharf Road where the walk starts
By car	Ellesmere is on the A528 from Shrewsbury and there is limited parking near to the Wharf Welshampton on the main A495 road between Whitchurch and Ellesmere. Park in the lay-by on the north side of the village
Refreshments	The Sun Inn in Welshampton. There are several cafes and inns at Ellesmere
Nearest Tourist Information Office	Ellesmere Visitor Centre, Mereside, Ellesmere Tel: 01691 622981

This walk can be undertaken from Ellesmere, an additional 5 miles of very pleasant canal towpath walk, or from Welshampton only as a much shorter loop.

Welshampton huddles around the busy A495 road but despite the traffic is a very pleasant village. The church is of interest and in the churchyard there's an unusual grave of a son of a Basuto chief,

Moshueshue, who died in 1824 having studied in these parts.

Ellesmere has always been an important market town in northern Shropshire and the wealth of past times is exhibited in the fine Georgian and Victorian buildings, which have been imprinted on an earlier medieval layout. A major change must have occurred when the canal network arrived and the big players of the time, led by the Duke of Bridgewater, invested heavily in putting Ellesmere at the centre of a canal map. It remains an important calling point for narrow boats on the Llangollen branch of the Shropshire Union Canal.

1. Start the walk from Wharf Road at the old wharf terminus. The Tesco supermarket stands to the right. Walk ahead on the canal towpath to a junction where you go over the bridge and then continue ahead. The walk soon leaves the crowds behind and there's a short tunnel (but torch not really needed for this one). You'll pass by Blake Mere and the next section, by Burns and Baysil woods, is beautifully tranquil. In all it is about 2½ miles to Colemere. You can divert here at Bridge 55 at Little Mill to walk around the country park if you prefer that option.

The wharf at Ellesmere

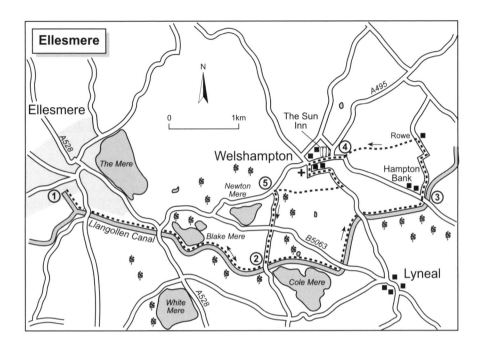

2. Otherwise, keep going along the canalside. There are glimpses through the trees to Cole Mere and a little chapel beyond. There are two more road bridges and then the canal runs alongside Lyneal Moss, on the opposite side before reaching Hampton Bridge. Here, you go under the bridge and then look for a little white gate on the left which exits into Rowe Lane.

3. Go right here and follow the lane to Orchard Cottage on the left. Just after, go left through a barred gate opposite Rowe Farm. Walk ahead through the field, then go through another gate beneath trees and ahead in the next field. The track exits onto a road at Balmer. Go right to walk facing the traffic. You soon reach Welshampton where you turn left to walk through the village to pass The Sun Inn.

4. This is the starting point for those wanting the shorter circular walk out of Welshampton (as the bus stops either side of the road here). Continue ahead to the church. Go left here and the lane soon leaves the village. As you approach a house go right over a stile into a field where horses are usually grazing. This is gently undulating

countryside with pools and woodland between pastures. Follow a hedge to the kissing gate and go through it. Turn right to follow the alternative path and then along the corralled path which climbs up a gate. Head slightly right down to a gateway and, once through, your way is slightly right, rising up a bank to a large oak and through a kissing gate by some holly. Walk ahead in the next field with the hedgerow to your right. Go through the gap and ahead again to drop down to a kissing gate to the right of a barred gate and to a road.

5. Turn left here along a lane which does not encourage traffic; there's a lovely green strip of grass down the middle. Go over a crossroads and continue down the lane to Bridge Number 55 at Little Mill. If you are on the short walk, follow instruction 2 onwards. If you are on the longer Ellesmere walk turn right for the return trip. There are, of course, opportunities to divert to The Mere, if this is preferred or simply walk back to The Wharf.

14. Far Forest

Easy to moderate walking, along woodland tracks; there are a few climbs. The highlights are the orchards in blossom and the Dowles Brook where you might see a heron take a fish.

Distance	6 miles (10km)
Allow	3 hours
Map	OS Explorer 204 Wyre Forest and Kidderminster
By bus	There is a regular daily bus service, 292 between Kidderminster and Ludlow
By car	Travel on the A4117 from Ludlow or the A456 from Kidderminster to the village. There is limited on street parking
Refreshments	The Plough in Far Forest or the local stores in the same village; 'Button Oak' in Button Oak
Nearest Tourist Information Office	The Library, Bridgnorth Tel: 01746 763257

The Wyre Forest, in the far south east of the county, is one of the few remaining Royal Hunting Forests to have survived as a large area of traditional woodland, rather than simply a name referring to a previous land use. Evidently, the Forest was well used by royalty during the Plantagenet and Tudor periods. Part of the forest is a National Nature Reserve designated by the Nature Conservancy Council, now English Nature, with a view to conserving it as a good example of native woodland rich in wildlife. The reserve is mainly based around the Dowles brook, which is also the county boundary, and is a superb section of the walk.

1. Start the walk at The Plough which is in Worcestershire. Opposite the Plough Inn go down Plough Lane. You come to a junction and here you

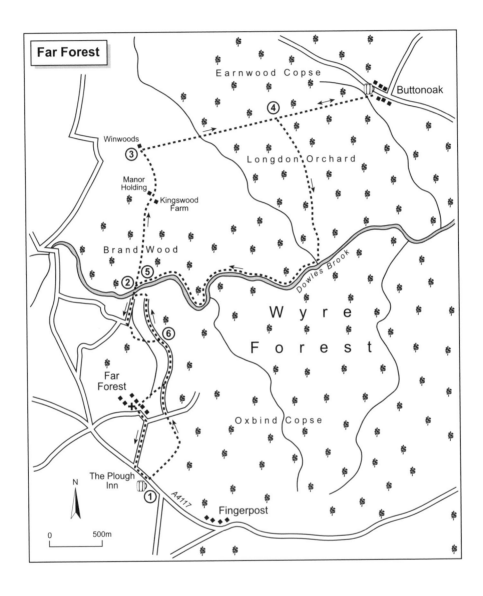

Far Forest

go left over a stile to walk alongside a garden to a second stile. Cross this and ahead through the field to exit into Sugar Lane. Keep ahead at the cross roads and at the next junction ahead again. The road leads by the Wyre Forest Holiday Village. The road runs through to Goodmoor Hill Farm only. You pass over the old railway line between Wooferton Junction to Bewdley, known as the Wyre Forest route. It was closed between Wooferton and Tenbury Wells in 1961 and the remainder of the route in 1962. You may hear the haunting sound of a steam engine whistle blowing on the walk; it is not this line! The enthusiasts back in the 1960s could not afford to re-open this one and selected the Severn Valley Railway instead. What a major success story it has been since those early days. The road descends, towards the farm. Cross a stile at the corner before the farm entrance. The path drops between hedges and bends left into the wood to drop down to meet another. Go right and cross the footbridge over the brook. You are now in Shropshire.

2. Once over the bridge walk to the T-junction and go left here to climb up the hillside of Brand Wood. At the next two crossroads keep ahead. The path begins to narrow and bends to a gate. Keep ahead as signposted as you have now joined the the GeoPark Way, a path from the River Severn to The Malverns, some 109 miles, which is designed to highlight geology and landscape. More details can be obtained by a google search 'Earth Heritage Trust'. Then, go left on a track where there's a house to your right and in twenty paces or so go right to pass Manor Holding. Keep to the right of the property along an enclosed path to cross a stile into a small field. Proceed through the barred gate and part way along the hedge, look for a gap in the hedge. This is your way; turn right so as to walk with the hedge to your right. Cross a stile by a barred gate onto a track.

Orchard apple blossom

3. Stay on this for a short while only, as you need to go right through the next barred gate on your right. Follow the field's edge on your left, through a gateway and then the path descends down a large field to a footbridge in the bottom left corner. Once over, go right and follow the green belt up the hillside of Corbets Park. You reach a major crossroads. You have a choice here; you can keep ahead and walk to the Button Oak public house at Button Oak (and retrace your steps to this point) or go right onto the forest track (which doubles as a National Cycle Route 45).

4. Go right on Route 45. Follow this, more or less ahead, as it descends for a mile to reach the valley of the Dowles Brook. At the junction keep ahead and as this track bends left to go over a bridge you head off right. Proceed ahead at the next junction, through wet ground and with the stream to your left. If you are fortunate you might see a heron catch fish on the river much to the annoyance of the local fishing community. The walk up the valley is about one mile and it may be wet in places.

5. You return to the footbridge where you may have paused on the way out. Go back over the bridge and into the woodland again. This time, go right over another bridge and up a bank. Join a track and at the far end of the dwelling go left on a path which skirts the garden and dips down to a stream. It is then a fairly hard climb back up the other side to Forest Dell.

6. Go right here and walk along the road to pass a junction on your left. Keep ahead and as the road bends left a little, look for a stile on the right. Go down this corralled path at the bottom of a traditional orchard. This is an area known for its small orchards; they really add character to this border landscape area. The path climbs up to a road. Go left and it bends right to ease up to the village hall on the main road. Go left to The Plough.

15. Gobowen

An easy walk, including a short section of Wat's Dyke, through gently rolling countryside mainly on paths but with some road walking at the start and end. The highlights are the beautifully restored Gobowen railway station and the Old Fort at Oswestry. Be prepared to get your feet wet crossing a stream.

Distance	5 miles (8km)
Allow	2-3 hours
Map	OS Explorer 240 Oswestry
By train	There is a daily service from Shrewsbury, Wrexham and Chester and direct services from several places beyond
By bus	There is a regular service from Ellesmere, Shrewsbury and Wrexham
By car	Oswestry is signposted from the A5 by-pass of the town. There are several car parks near to the centre. Gobowen has limited on street parking
Refreshments	There are shops and public houses in Gobowen
Nearest Tourist Information Office	Heritage Centre, Oswestry Tel: 01691 662753

1. Start from Gobowen Raliway Station. Go left and walk in the direction of Oswestry. Cross over the road and pass by a roundabout to a new estate. Turn next right to cross a bridge over the A5 road; all of this is not particularly pleasant but you are nearly off road. Once over the bridge walk along the road, facing the traffic; the road narrows. Not a particularly wonderful start to the walk but now it gets immeasurably better.

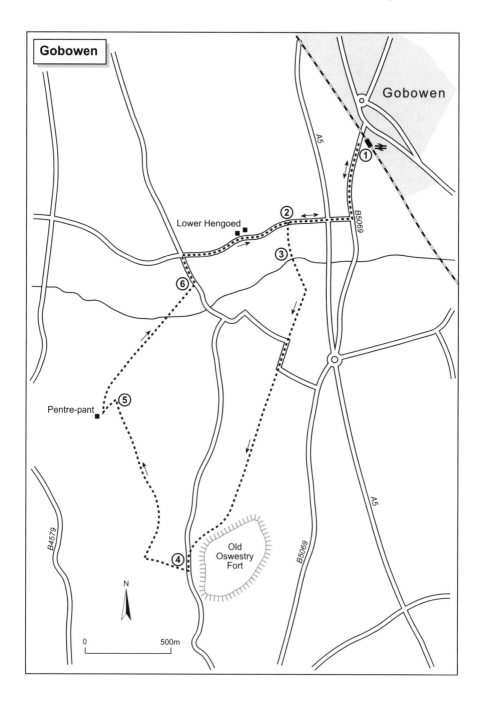

2. Before the road comes to a bend look for a stone marker on the other side. This is a well kept secret; your way through a little snicket to a stile. Cross this and head slightly right on the Wat's Dyke Way, which is a 61 mile long distance route between Maesbury and the River Dee in Flintshire. At the next boundary, cross a stile and head in a similar direction. Aim for a stile beyond an electric telegraph pole and to the right of a dwelling. Ignore the stile to the right beneath the oak tree. Go past the house to a road and to a stile, which you also cross.

3. Head slightly right to the far corner of the field. Go through the gate; keep ahead with the hedgerow to your left. Cross a stile and keep ahead until you reach a road. Go ahead and at the junction, keep ahead on the No Through Road at Pentre-Clawdd. Cross the stile by the barred gate with the farm to your right. Go slightly right to cross a stile by a barred gate. Keep ahead with the hedge to your left. From this point onwards you can see the Old Fort; it is not hard to imagine what it would have been like for an advancing army; an attack of the pallisade would not be for the faint hearted. Cross a stile beneath a tree and march onwards to the fort. Before you reach it bear right to walk along the perimeter fence to a bridle gate and a road.

4. Go left and by the car parking bay go right through a kissing gate and keep ahead along a permissive path to a stile on the right, which you cross. In the next field, go right across the field to cross a stile in a hedge. The landscape is more undulating, presumably postglacial deposits from a previous ice age. Cross the next stile and keep ahead to another beneath a large tree. Head up the bank then go forward to a barred gate. Go through it and aim for the house directly ahead. Follow the hedge through to a barred gate and a track.

5. Turn left to pass another dwelling with a tall hedge and just beyond look for a stile on the right. Go over this and walk along a corralled path to cross another stile. Head slightly right across the field to the left of a barred gate. Cross a stile by the water tank. Once across go through a barred gate and then head slightly left to a stile hidden in the bottom left corner of the field. Cross the stream but be prepared to step over stones or go through water. Cross a stile then walk through the next field in the direction of the houses, through a barred gate, and to a stile which leads onto a road.

6. Go left and at the crossroads turn right. Pass by the ornate Trewern. Unfortunately, the only route back is by road as the on level crossings of the A5 by footpath are lethal. Walk down the road to face the traffic but you may like to cross over where visibility is weaker. Go over the bridge crossing the A5 and retrace your steps into Gobowen. This last section may not be the best way to end the walk but take a look at the grand architecture of the railway station and it puts into perspective the legacy we are leaving in the early 21st century for future generations.

Old Fort, Oswestry

16. Hopton Heath to Craven Arms

This is an exquisite walk through a quiet part of the county. The highlights are Hopton Castle, as featured on the Tim Team series, and the pleasant walking in the Clun valley.

Distance	9 miles (15km)
Allow	4-5 hours
Map	OS Explorers 201 Knighton and Presteigne and 217 The Long Mynd and Wenlock Edge
By train	There is a daily service from Shrewsbury on the Heart of Wales line to Hopton Heath. This is a request stop so you will have to let the conductor guard know that you require Hopton Heath. All adds to the fun!
By bus	There is a bus 738/740 from Ludlow to Hopton Heath on Mondays to Saturdays. Less fun, but could be the best way to get there for those staying or living in Ludlow
By car	Hopton Heath is on the B4367 between Craven Arms and Bucknell. Parking is very limited near to the railway station
Refreshments	The Engine and Tender pub at Broome and The Kangaroo Inn at Aston-on-Clun
Nearest Tourist Information Office	Shropshire Hills Discovery Centre, Craven Arms Tel: 03456 789024 discovery.centre@shropshire.gov.uk

Hopton Heath is one of the least used stations in the country, let alone Shropshire. Let's change its fortune by notching up the number of arrivals. It serves a very rural community and, in particular, nearby Hopton Castle, which looks at its best in Spring when the daffodils are in full bloom. The castle is on private ground but you can obtain good views of the Norman keep from the road. It has witnessed many skirmishes through the centuries and especially in the English Civil War when the Parliamentarians were besieged by a large Royalist force ending in a deadly battle when the incumbents were routed.

Clunbury is one of the quietest villages according to Houseman in his oft quoted poem. The village is huddled around the parish church, which in turn overlooks the mill and the running waters of the River Clun. The River Clun is a European Special Area of Conservation. There have been projects to encourage the coppicing of the alders alongside the river banks near here. This serves to improve bankside habitats and to help with the improvement of spawning grounds for salmon and trout. The alders were planted originally for charcoal and clog production. In recent years charcoal production has been piloted. Let's hope that it can get on a commercial footing and help retain a habitat as well.

1. Start the walk from the station platform at Hopton Heath. There would have been a small goods yard here too in earlier times; a weighbridge and hut survives (private property). Walk up to the road, go left over the footbridge and turn left again to walk along the road to Hopton Castle with its wide verges. You approach a bend. You might be able to see the outline of Hopton motte, presumably a wooden fortress superseded by Hopton Castle. Look for steps up to a stile on the right. Cross the stile and head slightly left across the field to a holly bush. There's a gate on the left here, which you go through to return to the road. Walk on into the village where you'll pass a junction and see the castle at closer quarters.

2. In the village turn first right for Twitchen but at the corner go ahead up a drive which gives out into an enclosed track. This rises up to a stile. Cross it and in the field keep to the right of the old building, aiming for a stile beneath a large tree. Cross it and keep ahead with the hedge to your left. This leads to a stile in the field corner and you emerge onto a road.

3. Turn left and almost opposite is a stile. Cross this and head through the wood to a track. Go left to follow it but not for long. Be vigilant for you are looking for a marker post on the right. At this point leave the track and follow the path, which descends to the left down the hillside to a stile. Cross it and keep ahead alongside the wood to reach a stile.

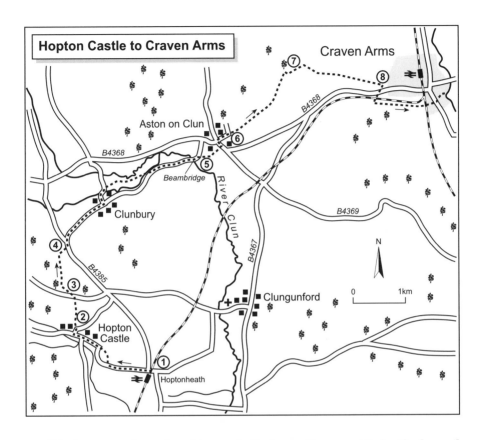

Climb over and now head towards the barn. Cross a stile by the barred gate. Proceed to the barn where you go through two barred gates (to left of building). Now keep ahead to cross the stream again and up to a stile which exits on to the B4385.

4. Cross with due care and go left then right along Twitchen Road to Clunbury. At the crossroads go left and pass the church, hall and old mill. The road leads over a bridge and where it bends left, go right through the first barred gate. Follow the hedge on your left ahead through the first of several riverside pastures. Pass through a gate and head slightly right between electric telegraph poles to a barred gate. Keep ahead to the stile adjacent to a barred gate; there's a barn to the right. Proceed in the same direction to cross another stile and then pass a dwelling to the left. Your way is onward to a stile by a gate and

you will find a footbridge over the River Clun leading to the road at Hill End

5. Turn left to walk to the few houses at a junction; this is Beambridge. Go left over the bridge which was erected in 1908 by Clun Rural District Council at a time when local authorities were local. About 100 metres up the road go right over a stile, as signposted, into a field. Cross the next stile and proceed onward to a barred gate and a bridle gate. Walk up the track to modern housing and follow Redwood Drive, which bends to the right to the main road in Aston-on-Clun (see walk 3).

6. Cross the road, turn left and at the junction go right to pass the Arbor Tree and a round house in Mill Street. The road soon bends left but you keep ahead on a track. Go over the stile by a gate to enter a field. Walk ahead but part way along look for a stile on the right and across a sunken lane, to cross another. Once through, go left and then keep ahead with the hedge to your left to the field corner. Cross the stile and go ahead in the next pasture to cross another and a small stream.

Hopton Castle

Keep ahead now; the hedge is to your right. The path becomes a track and runs beneath gorse banks to the left of dwellings at Oldfield.

7. The track runs by Oldfield Wood and exits at a barred gate into parkland. You will soon see the buildings of Sibdon Cardwood with their very own church. Keep ahead towards the hall but you will soon meet another path coming in from the cottage to your left. Turn right on this path and follow the waymark across the parkland to a stile beneath a large tree. Go slightly left to a kissing gate and cross a stile. Aim for the far left hand corner. Cross a stile here onto a back lane. Go over the road, cross a stile and head slightly left in the next field to the bottom left hand corner where you will find the next stile. Cross it and go right and keep ahead with the hedge to your right. Follow this until you reach a road, Watling Street.

8. There's a choice here. If you need to get back to the railway station pronto, then cross over the road and head slightly left for the new houses across the field. Cross a stile and walk along the drive to another stile. Cross this and head slightly right across a small pasture to exit on to the Clun Road. Go left and walk into town. Before the railway bridge go left and look for the path on the right to the station platforms. If you have more time available, then follow the Shropshire Way to the Shropshire Hills Discovery Centre. Go right along Watling Street and as it bends left keep ahead to the Clun Road. Go over and walk up Park Lane. After the railway bridge, go left over a stile by a gate. Walk ahead to the first boundary and then go slightly right to a stile by a gate and onward to a stile and a track. Walk down the track to houses and to the main A49 road. Cross over and The Shropshire Hills Discovery Centre is to your right. Time for tea?

17. Ironbridge

A walk through gentle countryside with one climb up Benthall Edge but otherwise no real gradients. Several points of interest on route.

Distance	6 miles (10km)
Allow	3 hours
Map	OS Explorer 242 Telford, Ironbridge and The Wrekin
By train	There is a daily train service to Telford from Shrewsbury and The West Midlands. The Gorge Connect bus runs to Ironbridge from Easter until the end of October at weekends
By bus	There is a daily bus, except Sundays, from Wellington and Bridgnorth, numbers 9 and 99. Several buses serve Ironbridge from Telford
By car	Ironbridge Gorge is well-signed from the A5 from Shrewsbury and the M54 from Wolverhampton. Travel through the land of a thousand roundabouts to the gorge. Car Parking available on both sides of The Iron Bridge
Refreshments	Plentiful supply in Ironbridge and also at Broseley
Nearest Tourist Information Office	The Toll House, Ironbridge Tel: 01952 884391 tic@ironbridge.org.uk

As you stand on the world's first Iron Bridge it is hard to believe that this is where it all happened in the eighteenth century, the trigger for the Industrial Revolution. It was not a revolution in the usual sense of the word but a string of technological and economic achievements over the decades which changed Britain from an agrarian society to an industrial and urban nation.

The entire area is a living museum of those early days but in particular the Ironbridge Gorge Museums each tell a story of importance. This group of museums and other sites are all in close proximity of the Ironbridge Gorge itself and there's more than one can see in just a day. Stay a few days or return time and time again as there's always something new to see at this UNESCO World Heritage Site.

1. Start your walk at the Iron Bridge. Walk over the bridge and go right along the old Great Western Railway track bed, now set out as a trail and part of The Severn Valley Walk. The line was built to   link Kidderminster and Shrewsbury and survived a hundred years until the era of Beeching cuts. Continue ahead towards the power station. On your way you'll see the results of the re-introduction of coppicing in this wood. This is the cutting back of shrubs and younger trees every 10 years or more so that shoots become more prolific and the amount of wood larger in the long term.

2. As you approach the fence to the Ironbridge B power station, with a full frontal of the cooling towers (you gain a sense of scale from this viewpoint), go left over a stile and left again as the path rises. At a junction, where a bench stands, go right as signposted to Benthall. You come to another fork and you keep right. Climb up through the Benthall Edge wood, ignoring a left fork. You will see open pasture to the right but the informal path by the fence is not the route! You rise up to join a track. Follow this as it climbs up to curve sharp left; it is signposted to Benthall. This climbs up to a gate on the right. Go through it and walk straight on to Benthall Hall Farm.

3. You pass to the right of a farm and continue ahead to see the church and Benthall Hall. You come to a small gate as the track becomes a road. Go through and walk ahead through parkland, with the Hall directly to your left. The Hall, built in the 1530s, is a fine Tudor Manor and family home of the Benthall family. It contains some marvellous furniture from previous centuries. As you walk by, you'll notice the very distinctive stone-mullioned windows and moulded brick chimneys which add character to the house.

   Before the next gate go right along a the line of trees. Go through a kissing gate to rough ground. Proceed ahead with the fence on the right to another stile. Cross this and go left, passing to the left of a small pool. Go through gates into the next small pasture. Keep ahead

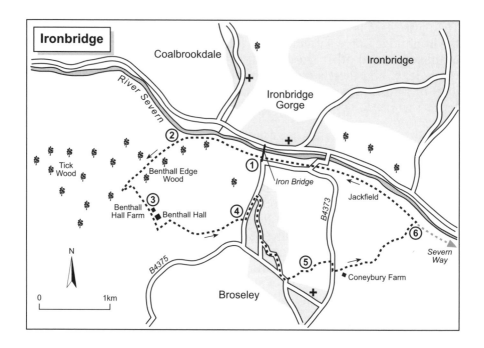

now with hedge to the right. Before it becomes a track, however, cross the stile on the right and another soon after to walk alongside a garden wall and fence to a lane.

4. Nearby in Broseley, many of the old pathways, known locally as jitties, have been cleared and signed. It is easy to get lost down them but if you are walking in this area it is worth wandering around these nooks and crannies. Go right on the lane and then left to descend and then climb Barratt's Hill. Walk up High Street into Broseley centre. Continue through the town to turn left down Dark Lane, opposite Victoria Hall dating from 1867. The famous Iron Master, John Wilkinson, lived and worked in Broseley. He commissioned the first iron boat, The Trial, built in 1787 and developed numerous applications for iron including being buried himself in an iron coffin! The house, The Lawns, where Wilkinson once lived is nearby in Church Street. It is still a private residence with a very large collection of porcelain and pottery which is open to the public on certain afternoons.

5. As the road curves left, just beyond the first large house on the right, go right down a track, which is signed. Follow the bridleway as it descends into the valley, Ignore any left or right turnings. Go right at the road and then left at the next junction signposted to Coneybury and Woodhouse Farms. Continue ahead to join a bridleway into the wood. At the end of the wood go straight ahead. Go through a gate and continue to descend, ignoring any side turnings, passing through another gate into the delightful and unexpected Corbett's Dingle. At a junction, follow the path ahead, keeping alongside the stream at first but then moving away until you eventually pass through a gateway with a house on your left.

6. Continue along a tarmac road to face an old brick-built railway bridge. From here you have a choice – either way involves some road walking. The speediest return route is to go up the steps on your right before the bridge. At the top of the steps, turn left and continue towards Jackfield along The Severn Valley Way. The first part of this route is along the track bed of the Great Western Railway. Then you meet the road. Continue ahead to pass The Jackfield Tile Museum, to your left. The road cross an old level crossing and here you can walk along the old railway track bed and to the Iron Bridge.

18. Knighton to Bucknell

A moderate walk with one steep climb out of Stowe to Holloway Rocks where there are superb views. This is a linear walk between the railway stations of Knighton and Bucknell.

Distance	**7 to 8 miles (11 to 12km)**
Allow	**4 hours**
Map	**OS Explorer 201 Knighton and Presteigne**
By train	**Knighton and Bucknell are stations on the Heart of Wales line. There are four trains each way on a Monday to Saturday, with two trains on Sundays**
By bus	**There is a bus service 738/740 between Ludlow and Knighton on Mondays to Saturdays. There is a bus stop by the entrance to the railway station to alight (from either Ludlow or Knighton) and it is the best stop for return trips in both directions**
By car	**Bucknell is on the B4367 from Craven Arms to Knighton. It is also a mile off the A4113 from Ludlow to Knighton. There is not much on-street car parking in the village, another reason for catching the train**
Refreshments	**There are cafés and pubs in Knighton and two pubs, The Baron of Beef and the Sitwell Arms in Bucknell. There are also two or three shops in the village**
Nearest Tourist Information Office	**Offa's Dyke Heritage Centre, Knighton Tel: 01547 528753 oda@offasdyke.demon.co.uk**

The walk starts at Knighton railway station and finishes at Bucknell. Catch the train to Knighton for the start of the walk. Arrive at Bucknell in time for the train or bus ride to Knighton. It is only a short ride away. It is even better if you travel all of the way to Knighton by bus or train. This interesting borderland town is well worth exploration. Known in Welsh as Tref-y-Clawdd, meaning the 'Town of the Dyke', Knighton is the only settlement of any size actually situated on the dyke itself. The path cuts through the town and beneath an archway by the Knighton Hotel.

Knighton is very much a market town. Thursday is probably the busiest day for the traditional shops huddled around the market place but there's also a small but vibrant farmers market on the second and fourth Saturday of the month. The marvel, of course, is the dominant Victorian Clock Tower, nestled between two roads; it is a real landmark in the town.

1. The walk commences from Knighton station which happens to be just in Shropshire. From the station platform 1 walk up steps, go right to cross the footbridge and right again. Opposite is the beautifully corrugated main depot of Owen's Motors, a long standing company in

Walking near Bucknell

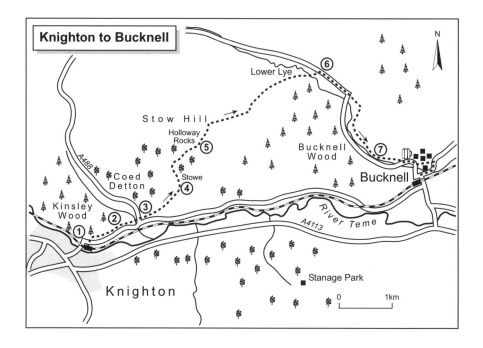

the town. You have guessed right; the author is a corrugated iron aficionado. Walk along the main A488 road but only for 100 metres before crossing into Kinsley Wood to join a path which slopes upwards into the mixed woodland rich in ash, beech and oak. Follow this delightful route through the wood until you reach a forestry track at a 'U' bend. Descend as indicated on the waymark then turn left to rise to another 'U' bend.

2. There are steps down to a stile beneath a tree. Cross it to enter a large field. Your way is across the field, slightly left, to a stile leading onto the main A488. The stile is the landmark to head for but you have to cross a footbridge immediately beforehand. This cannot be seen until you are some way over the field.

3. Cross the road and go through the gateway. Continue ahead with the hedge to your left to the next gateway. Go through this and you are now walking through pleasant fields with the hedge to your right. It is hard to believe that this was once an old roadway to Stowe; it has obviously lost its significance in recent decades. The route is easy to

follow through a succession of fields, always keeping the hedge to your right. The path begins to rise and when you are in need of a breather look over your shoulder. There's an impressive view of Knighton, sitting solidly above the banks of the Teme in the gap between Ffridd and Panpunton hills. It is easy to see from here why it was such a strategic gap town, no doubt the subject of many skirmishes in past times. The path leads up to a barred gate situated on a brow above Stowe. There is a superb view of the hamlet and church. This neat little church contains lovely stained glass windows, suggested by the famous architectural historian, Nicholas Pevsner, as being 'art nouveau' in style.

4. At this point, your way is slightly left down the hillside (rather than through the barred gate immediately on your left). Go through the bridle gate and now aim for a point just to the left of the cottages where you cross a stream and join a track. This passes to the left of the cottages and by a melancholy looking building adjacent to a pocket of wood. The path rises to a barred gate to enter the wood and rises up to join a more prominent track up to Holloway Rocks. It curves right and left as it climbs up a dry valley to Holloway Rocks, a niche in the outcrop of Stow Hill. This is a route which has, no doubt, given many a drover a hard time in inclement weather. Rest awhile at the top. The views across the Teme valley to the Radnor Hills are splendid and you'll need time to recover from the climb!
Once at the top continue ahead across this large and open field. Your landmark is a stile which leads into the plantation but do not go over it. Instead, turn right and keep ahead as the plantation drops away to the left. The track soon descends, passing a secluded pool on your left. At the next gateway go left and pass through other gates on a track which begins to descend towards Vron farm.

5. There are good views of the Redlake Valley and exceptional view of Caer Caradoc, a relatively small Iron Age camp but at over 1200 feet, providing a strong defensive position. Could this have been the site of Caracticus's last brave stand against the Romans before his capture? Some say the event might have taken place at the fort on nearby Coxall Knoll. It is possible, of course, but most writers suggest that the location was Caer Caradoc, near Church Stretton. You will also see the hamlet of Chapel Lawn in the valley, literally meaning a clearing in the wood where a chapel can be found.

The view from Holloway Rocks

Follow the track down to pass Vron farm, then continue into a sunken lane ahead. This descends to Lower Lye Farm where you pass ahead through the yard. Walk down to the River Redlake, crossed by a footbridge, and to a lane beyond.

6. Go right on the lane and follow the road to a point just before the bridge. Go over a stile on the left and follow the river bank, right, to a stile in the field boundary. Cross the stile and head slightly right up the bank as the river meanders away to the right. Cross the stile and join a more prominent path in the wood. Go right along this lovely green track, which is easy to follow. What a contrast to the wildness of the terrain near Holloway Rocks.

7. You come to the outskirts of Bucknell where the track meets a lane. Continue ahead on the road to a junction. Go left. Follow this through the sizeable village, passing by the Baron of Beef public house (open lunchtimes and evenings) and to the church. Go left by the churchyard and at the next road junction go right by the Sitwell Arms to the railway station (usually open evenings only but also at lunchtimes at the weekend). Then, it is a matter of a few steps back to the railway station of Bucknell with its magnificent station house and single platform. This is a far cry from when there were two platforms, a coal depot and sidings for timber and other agricultural goods and numerous staff to keep the place going.

19. Llanymynech

A borderland walk winding in and out of Wales along Llanymynech hill, with a few steep climbs and the occasional flying golf ball.

Distance	4.5 miles (7-8km)
Allow	2-3 hours
Map	OS Explorer 240 Oswestry
By bus	There is a regular bus service 72 on Monday-Saturday from Oswestry with a limited service, D74, from Shrewsbury
By car	Llanymynech is on the main A483 from Oswestry to Welshpool. From Shrewsbury travel along the A5 then the B4396 and B4398. There is a limited amount of on-street parking off the A483, which is to be avoided
Refreshments	There are a number of public houses in the village
Nearest Tourist Information Office	Heritage Centre, Oswestry Tel: 01691 662753

Llanymynech residents must have cursed the Boundary Commission for the village straddles the England-Wales border and so does this walk. The hills here are predominantly used for leisure now but were once the scene of heavy quarrying. This was so even in earlier times for it is estimated that the Romans had copper mines here and, in later centuries, the hills have been worked for limestone. Much of the old mineral workings, railways and many canal wharfs have gone or are overgrown. Nevertheless, you will see some of this heritage of interest on this short circular ramble.

1. Start by The Cross Keys Hotel by the main crossroads in the centre of the village. Walk up towards Llanymynech hill on the right hand side of the road. Go down steps to the canal and if you look over to the right you'll see the transhipment wharfs where much of the limestone was shipped out in the last century. Go left under the bridge and walk ahead on the towpath of the Montgomery Canal

2. Go right into Carreghofa Lane and as it bends right look for a track on the right. Go right along it to pass by bungalows and this bends right over an old railway bridge and into a field. Keep left to enter a field by

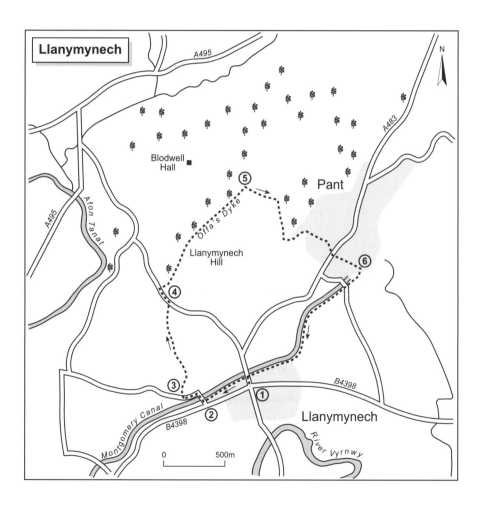

a barred gate. Follow the hedge to the corner and then head towards the farm to a barred gate leading onto a track.

3. Go right here to climb up a green lane. It dips to a ford then climbs steeply between gardens and dwellings. On reaching the road go left to pass by a group of houses at Fron-goch where it becomes a track. Go right here up a bridleway, opposite a barred gate at a farm.

4. Continue up this track to a gate. Now, keep going uphill through the woodland. You come out onto a golf course where you go left on Offa's Dyke Path twisting along the edge by the remains of the dyke. As you look over the edge into Wales you can understand why the dyke utilised this hillside. The path reappears onto the edge of the golf course and keeps to the left-hand fence for a while before being waymarked into the rough again. It then begins to descend, crossing a stile, and through scrub. This obscures the view over Wales. You will probably see, however, a large farm below in the valley. You come to a junction. Go right here through a thickly wooded section, almost like a tunnel of darkness. Do not go left but keep ahead to a stile, which brings you onto the course, once again.

5. Cross two greens with care so as not to collide with one of those little white missiles. Notice the remaining earthworks of a hill fort to the right. Continue ahead on a green track and be guided by three marker posts. Proceed downhill to a gate by a house. Go through the gate, turn left and then right along narrow lanes. At the wider Briggs Road, turn right to walk down to the main road by the Cross Guns public house. Cross over and walk down a narrow road which runs ahead. On reaching the junction with Starcarreg Lane go right along Storey Steps, which drop down to a small meadow to walk past an old kiln. Go left on the road to the bridge.

6. This leads to the tow-path of the Montgomeryshire canal, more properly known as The Ellesmere Canal. Go left. Unfortunately, after a breach in 1936 The London Midland and Scottish Railway ensured that it was abandoned by the 1940s. It is amazing that so much has survived and restoration is taking place along certain sections but very slowly. Go up the steps to the main road and turn left for the centre of the village.

20. Ludlow

An easy ramble with superb views of Clee Hill and through Caynham Iron Age Camp.

Distance	8 miles (13km)
Allow	4 hours
Map	OS Explorer 203 Ludlow and Cleobury Mortimer
By train	Ludlow is on the Marches line and enjoys a regular daily service
By bus	You might want to start your walk at The Eco Park at Sheet (point 2) rather than to walk from town (the urban bit) so you can catch bus 702/3 from the Mraket Square. They run every 15 minutes on Mondays to Saturdays
By car	The Eco Park is situated on the A49 by-pass road
Refreshments	Plentiful supply of cafés, shops and inns in Ludlow
Nearest Tourist Information Office	Castle St, Ludlow Tel: 01584 875053 info@ludlow.org.uk

No wonder A.E. Houseman had his ashes brought back to St Laurence's church in Ludlow, for it is one of the loveliest places in The Marches. It has been a sought-after place since the great days of wool trading when fortunes were made from the sale of fleeces by diligent merchants. Patterns of trade have changed somewhat and tourism has become more important than hitherto. There are plenty of events throughout the year from the Food Festival to the Green Fair. The latter reflects a vibrant environmental movement in the town, headed by Ludlow 21 (google it),

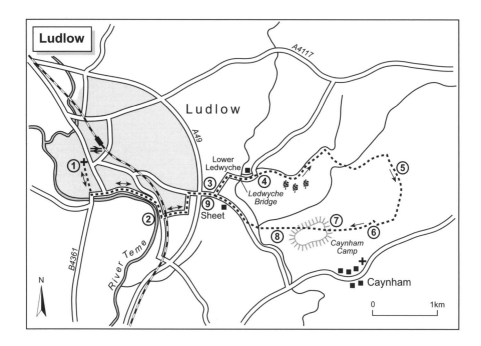

which seeks to encourage a wide range of green initiatives including bus and train walks!

Look at the town from any direction and you cannot fail to notice the prominence of the castle, particularly when arriving by train from the Hereford direction. This Norman fortress has withstood the ravages of time well; it is open to the public and is a centre piece during the lively annual Ludlow Festival.

Narrow medieval passages radiate from this quarter and yet close by there are many fine examples of Georgian townhouses, most of which are listed. Needless to say, there are a several guide books singing the praises of Ludlow and virtually all of the walking routes from the town are in a publication so why not try a few? Add this little ramble to the itinerary and you have the makings of a good weekend. You simply cannot do justice to Ludlow in less time.

1. Start the walk from the church of St Laurence by the Butter Market. Walk down Broad Street opposite and through the last remaining town gateway along Lower Broad Street to Ludford Bridge where the handsome Charlton Arms stands over the water. Go left at the junction

and cross over to take a look at the horseshoe weir, one of several constructed on the River Teme hereabouts. As the road bends left into Old Street, you keep ahead along Temeside (the path is on the other side). As you approach the corner leading into Weeping Cross, walk back over to go right along a continuation of Temeside to reach a junction.

2. Go right and walk up a steeper climb to a second junction where you cut left to proceed up Foldgate Lane. This gives out at Tuffins supermarket. Go left and right to skirt it and reach a pedestrian crossing over the A49 road. Once over, keep ahead along Sheet Road.

3. On the left is a junction where there are two bus stops. This is where the Park and Ride bus (702/703) users start the walk. Either way, walk ahead into Sheet village. Go first left into a lane signposted to Henley. Pass by the electricity sub-station and through a wood at Ledwyche.

4. Rise up to a corner and by the old mill pool and go right here on a track between the hedge and field (ignore the turning to the right).

Ludlow Castle from Whitcliffe Common

Pass through Ledwyche covert and ahead with woodland on the left. You reach the next field boundary and your way is to the right walking with the hedge on the right, across a stream but still ahead. Cross a stile by an oak tree and head slightly left to go over a small bridge. Keep left but move away from the stream and covert to go through a bridle gate. Now proceed slightly left to climb a stile next to a gate. Make your way, slightly right, up the field where there's a stile in the right hand corner. Cross it and go ahead into the next field where you rise up with the hedge to your right. There's a good view of Clee Hill from here.

5. Keep ahead at the junction proceeding to a barred gate into a pasture. Now, go ahead again to a stream and through a bridle gate. Head slightly right across a large field to look for a stile at a mid-point. Continue in a similar direction with a dwelling as a landmark in the distance. You meet a cross path as you approach the corner (as Caynham is a parish with many paths). Go right onto it to trees where a hidden paths dips down a gully to a stream and climbs up again.

6. Head slightly right over a field to a hedge where a stile is crossed. Go right to follow the field's edge to the top right corner. Cross a stile and head slightly left to another stile by several small trees. Go over the stile and bear slightly right to another stile in a hawthorn hedge. Keep ahead to the top right corner where you will see the ramparts of Caynham Camp. At the summit you approach this ancient camp at a gap in the ramparts and to a stile adjacent to a gate. The camp is a very good example of an Iron Age site; the ramparts can be seen quite clearly surrounding its eight acres.

7. Cross a stile, a track and another stile by a gate. Enter the grassy enclave of the camp but keep right to cross a stile beneath trees. The path cuts down the hillside and bends left through the wooded embankment. It exits by way of a stile and runs through scrub land and between hawthorns to join a hedge. Keep ahead to meet a green track and head slightly right down to a stile by a gate.

8. Aim in a similar direction in the next field to cross a stile about 20 metres to the left of a large oak. Once over, head down to a footbridge and in the next field head slightly right to climb up a stile in a hedge. This leads to a road. Go right and follow this to the village of Sheet

Titterstone Clee Hill

and the turning to the Eco Park where there's a bus (702/3) to town on Mondays to Saturdays until early evening.

9. The path crosses the main A49 and after the turning for Tuffins supermarket go left along a tarmac path which leads to the equally narrow Foldgate Lane. Follow this down to a bridge over the railway and a junction with Steventon New Road. Turn right and then left at the bottom of the bank into Temeside. This joins Weeping Cross Lane and you need to turn left here and left again at the next junction. Before Ludford Bridge, turn right into Lower Broad Street to walk up to the centre of town. Turn left at the top for the Market Square.

21. Market Drayton

Easy walking along tracks, canal tow-path (one section is very wet) and across fields.

One highlight is the canal architecture and rich wildlife of the deep cuttings of the Shropshire Union canal. Another is the charming village of Cheswardine.

Distance	10 miles (16km)
Allow	5 hours
Map	OS Explorer 243 Market Drayton, Loggerheads and Eccleshall
By bus	There is a daily express X64 service between Hanley and Shrewsbury. There are also buses from Telford on Mondays to Saturdays
By car	Market Drayton is on the A53 from Newcastle-under-Lyme to Shrewsbury and the A41 (and A529) from Wolverhampton
Refreshments	Market Drayton has several cafés, shops and inns. The Four Alls inn and restaurant is on the route as is the shop at Tyrley Locks and there are the Wharf pub near Cheswardine and two pubs in the village – The Fox and Hounds and Red Lion
Nearest Tourist Information Office	Clive Library, Cheshire Street, Market Drayton Tel: 01630 653119

Market Drayton is a North Shropshire market town known for the baking of gingerbread and the association with the young Clive of India in the 19th century. Its narrow streets spill out from the large and interesting church of St Mary and there are a fair number of half timbered houses

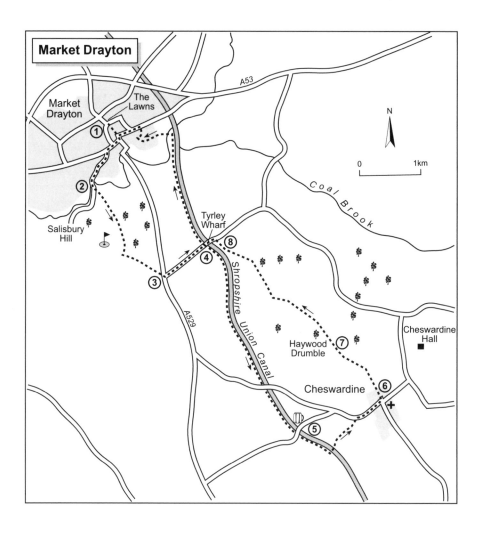

remaining, particularly in Shropshire Street. The town was devastated by fire in 1651 and the old fire bells still hang at the top of the traditional Buttercross. Visit Market Drayton on a Wednesday or Saturday when the street market brings the town very much to life.

Cheswardine is just in Shropshire but this has not always been the case. It is mentioned as 'Ciseworde' in the Domesday Book and listed under Staffordshire. More than one writer suggests that the name is related to cheese making and dairying is still important in the area, although most of it is destined for a large yoghurt manufacturer nearby. A local Cheswardine baker still holds an original recipe for gingerbread. Some say that it definitely has aphrodisiac properties so stock up if you find some. Do take care not to eat too much before the walk!

1. Start from Towers Lawn where there's a bus station and toilets. Go left along Queen Street which becomes pedestrianised. On reaching High Street go right into Shropshire Street and as Frogmore Street bends off to the right keep ahead. Go next left down Kiln Bank Road. Cross over Walkmill Road. Go left again over Walkmill Bridge, under which flows the River Tern.

2. Turn left again by an old house into Sandy Lane. Pass by a modern bungalow and the lane climbs through pleasant scenery. Take a look back at Market Drayton, perched on an edge above the river valley. Salisbury Hill is to your right, chronicled as the grounds where the Yorkists amassed before the bloody battle of Blore Heath, a few miles up the road. Can you imagine the scene? The lane rises by the entrance to Home Farm and then, beyond a cottage, there is a junction. Go left to the Four Alls Public House. Exit onto the road by the hostelry.

3. Cross the main road and walk down the road to Tyrley Locks, which are in Staffordshire. Go down the steps to the towpath and go right. The Shropshire and Union Canal, known affectionately as 'The Shroppie' was built in the 1820s and 30s and was one of the last great narrow boat canals. Thomas Telford held to his belief that it could retain heavy traffic between Ellesmere Port and The Midlands so as to stave off the competition from the emergent railways. The Shroppie was also one of the most rural of canal networks. This section of towpath highlights Telford's engineering sophistication with cuttings and embankments being the order of the day rather than following the

contours too closely. It is now a conservation area to reflect its importance as an architectural masterpiece.

4. There's a good two miles of towpath walking. You soon reach a deep cutting with high and splendidly arched bridges. You can smell the dankness here; it is so still. The water is constantly dripping down the walls embroidered in a rich and undisturbed vegetation and there's a constancy of birdsong to remind you of the biodiversity here. The superbly engineered bridges punctuate this stretch. They were exacted in the most detailed proportion so as to captivate the eye of the early boatman and the would-be traveler. Be warned, however, that the towpath is in poor condition in places and you'll need to wade through water and possibly some mud. It can be slow going but it's worth every moment. Be careful not to hug the canal edging stones for a loss of balance could lead to an unscheduled dip in the canal.

5. Pass by the Wharf Tavern at Goldstone (opposite bank) and continue ahead to reach the next bridge, number 54, where you peel off to the right. Go left over the bridge and you will see a mooring to your right. However, your way is through the trees on the left. Head slightly right through the covert; go through a gateway. There's a way-mark guiding the walker in a similar direction and hence aiming for the top left corner of the wood. Cross a stile here and walk up the field with the hedge to your left. Go through the barred gate and ahead again to a kissing gate. Continue along the hedge by a pool to a stile onto the road. Go right for the village of Cheshwardine. The public houses are situated in the main street.

6. At the corner by the church, go left along Lawn lane. The lane bends to the left but keep ahead and this becomes an un-surfaced track which gives out into a field. Choose the footpath which runs slightly left to cross diagonally to the far left corner. Cross a stile and footbridge and walk through the wood. Then cross a stile and keep ahead along a field's edge. At the end, cross a stile which leads into a covert. The path curves left and right by a pool to exit by way of a stile. Proceed ahead now with a hedge to your right to an opening into a new field. Keep ahead, with the hedge now on your left to skirt a pool. Cheswardine Park farm is across the field to your right. Aim for an oak tree. Keep ahead with the hedge to your left.

7. Cross a stile to enter Haywod Drumble. The path bends to the left and exits by way of a footbridge. Once over, go left and walk along the field's edge to the wood. Ignore the footbridge on the left. Keep ahead, along the field's edge to re-enter a wood by a footbridge and leave by one too. Now aim for an oak tree ahead and walk in that direction until you reach the field's edge. Go left to follow the line of trees to a track. Cross this and proceed directly ahead to a footbridge. Go over this and walk ahead again across a field to a stile which you cross. Head slightly left to follow the left hand edge of the field ahead to a stile and barred gate leading onto the road at Tyrley Locks.

8. Go left and walk up to the locks where you re-join the canal towpath, but this time walk in the opposite direction down the locks. You come to an elevated stretch as you approach Market Drayton once again. As you reach a large bridge over a road, go left down steep steps to the lane and then walk ahead towards the town on Berrisford Road. At the junction by the school grounds, go right and then left again at the main road back to the town centre.

22. Morville

A gentle walk along a valley of the Mor Brook but with one hard climb en route to Upton Cressett. The highlights include the Morville and Upton Cressett halls.

Distance	4 miles (6-7km)
Allow	2 hours
Map	OS Explorer 218 Wyre Forest and Kidderminster
By bus	There is a regular daily service, bus 436/7 between Shrewsbury and Bridgnorth
By car	Morville is situated on the A458 between Bridgnorth and Much Wenlock. There is some space for parking alongside the main road
Refreshments	The Acton Arms, Morville
Nearest Tourist Information Office	The Library, Listley St, Bridgnorth Tel: 01746 763357

Morville, lying in the Mor Brook valley, is a pleasant village with a hall dating from Elizabethan times but with extensive alterations in Georgian times. Morville church stands in the grounds nearby. It is said that two women and five horses were killed here in 1118 at the consecration ceremony. There was once a priory in the vicinity but there are no visible remains. However, the village retains a defunct whipping post and a pound.

1. Start the walk by the Acton Arms. Cross the road, with real care, to the steps and along a path running through the edge of a garden. There's a gate on your right across to the churchyard and then strike left towards the Mor Brook. Cross the stile and footbridge to continue on

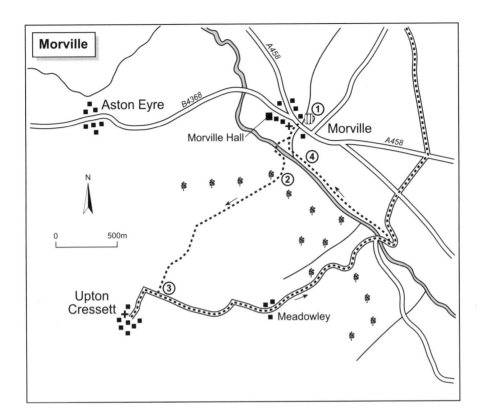

the riverside for a few paces then go slightly right up to a gate to enter Aston Hill wood.

2. Climb up the hillside ahead. The path rises remorselessly up the hill to exit at a stile into a large field. Head slightly right across the field to a corner where the path crosses a bridleway, i.e. across the track and ahead in a similar direction to a stile in the next hedge. Cross this and go left to walk down the field. From this point you will see Upton Cresset Hall and church. The hall dates from the 16th century and sits on the site of an earlier manorial building. There are also remains of a moat and old fishpond as this was a far bigger settlement in medieval times. It is now a private residence. Where the field indents, head slightly right across the field to the next corner. Walk down the hedge to a stile onto the road.

3. Go left on the lane and walk to the hamlet of Meadowley. From there onwards the lane descends to Lye Bridge. Once over, go left in the field and up the bank by the brambles, and then within a few metres, turn left. Your way is ahead, always keeping a parallel line on the bank near to the brook and then, after the next field boundary, through a waterside pasture.

4. Pass by the sewerage works once again and retrace your steps to the church. From here there are two alternatives. Either return to the Acton Arms as on the outward section or return by way of the hall. From the corner of the churchyard continue ahead to the left-hand building of the hall and then go right along the access road to the main road, passing directly in front of the hall.

23. Much Wenlock

A delightful walk along the limestone scarp slope of Wenlock Edge. There are some climbs and the highlight is the Edge itself.

Distance	**6-7 miles (11km)**
Allow	**3-4 hours**
Map	**OS Explorer 217 The Long Mynd and Wenlock Edge**
By bus	**There is a regular daily bus service, the 436/7, from Shrewsbury and Bridgnorth**
By car	**Much Wenlock is on the A458 road from Shrewsbury to Bridgnorth. It is also on the B4376 from Ironbridge. There is off-street car parking in town**
Refreshments	**Much Wenlock has several places to eat and drink**
Nearest Tourist Information Office	**The Museum, The Square, Much Wenlock Tel: 01952 727679**

Much Wenlock is as pleasant as it sounds. Its compact centre is full of interesting buildings which, in turn, house many traditional shops and inns. The Priory was established in 1080 and has had considerable influence over the growth of the settlement. The medieval structure of the town remains today and the local museum reflects the fortunes of Much Wenlock in past centuries in a series of interesting displays.

This small town can also lay claim to being one of the influences in the regeneration of Olympic Games in the twentieth century. Dr Penny Brookes established the Wenlock Olympian Society in 1850 and in the 1860s competitors came from all over England to participate in the Wenlock Games. Dr Brookes went on to campaign for physical education in schools.

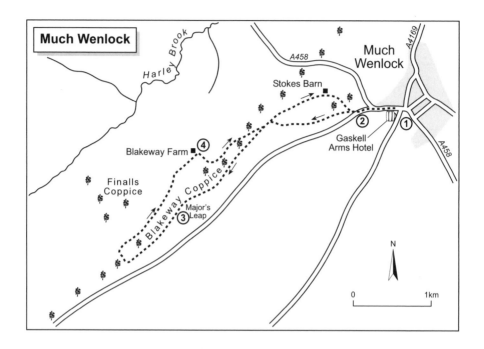

1. Start the walk at the Gaskell Arms Hotel, once an old coaching inn. Look out for the notices on the walls. Continue ahead along Victoria Road to rise up towards Wenlock Edge. The path is on the right-hand side of the road, elevated at times, and offering a good view of the old pound. Cross over to pass by Birchfield garage.

2. Go left onto Church Stretton Road and then turn first right, signposted to Blakeway Hollow. The metalled road gives out to a track; go over the stile next to the gate. Walk up the track and on reaching a junction keep left and then ahead to Blakeway Coppice and Presthouse. When the tree cover is not too extensive, you can see Hughley church and village to the left. A.E. Houseman immortalised Hughley in *The Shropshire Lad*. Part way along you will come to a waymark indicating the Major's Leap path. Climb up to join a path and go right to walk above the old Lea Quarry workings.

3. Look out for a right turn, sign-posted 'Shropshire Way' to Presthouse. This descends the hillside to join a more prominent woodland track.

Keep ahead to reach a junction. Go right as sign-posted to Blakeway Farm. This descends to a junction where you take the lower path and is very muddy in places. Another track joins the path, which soon reaches a gate into a pasture beneath the Edge. Go ahead to the barred gate and in to the next field. Head slightly left to the bridle gate at the bottom and go right on the track to Blakeway Farm.

4. Pass by the farm and just after turn right as signposted 'Ippikins Way' go up into the wood and keep left at the junction. Soon after, rise up a sunken track to reach a junction which you encountered on the outward leg. Keep ahead and as the track bends right proceed over a stile into a field. Walk along the hedge on your left to cross a stile into the next field. Now keep slightly right to a stile located to the right of a barred gate. Follow the track to pass by a barn and through a bridle gate. Then look for a stile on the left. Cross this and go right through a bridle gate. The path descends to Blakeway Hollow where you go left to retrace your steps into Much Wenlock.

24. Myddle

Easy walking across fields including a beautiful sandstone edge.

Distance	5 miles (8km)
Allow	3 hours
Map	OS Explorer 241 Shrewsbury
By bus	There is a daily bus 501 from Shrewsbury to Myddle
By car	Myddle is north of Shrewsbury on the A528 road to Ellesmere. There is a limited amount of on-street car parking
Refreshments	The Red Lion Inn is a focal point. There is also a village store
Nearest Tourist Information Office	Rowley's House, Barker Street Tel: 01743 281200

Beyond the church, on private land, stands the last remnant of Myddle Castle which fell into ruins during the 16th century. The settlement surrounding this fortress has nevertheless remained. It is a village sprawling along the road, which climbs the impressive sandstone edge to the main road and there are one or two handsome houses near to the church. The Red Lion public house is a central point for the community and, conveniently, the starting point for this walk.

1. From the Red Lion go left to walk uphill, towards the main road. Keep ahead as the road bends right to walk up steps to the right of the elevated brick built house, to Myddle Hill. Cross the main road and go over the stile into a very large field. The boundaries have obviously been grubbed in recent years and this expanse can often be in crop. However, keep ahead on a well worn path to pass by the small pool on your left and head towards a kissing gate. Go through this and go right along the hedge until you reach a bridle gate leading into a wood.

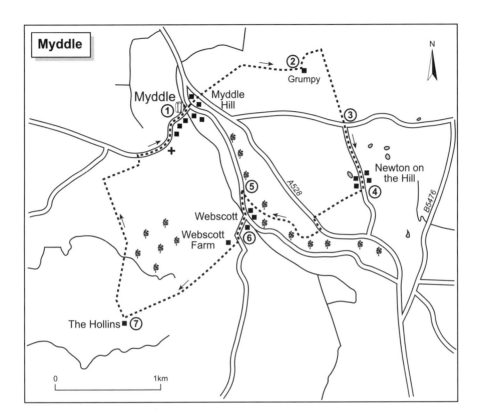

2. The path reaches a lane by a house at a place, believe it or not, called Grumpy. Go right onto the road and then left along the bridleway, which is signposted. After a quarter of a mile, be vigilant for you are looking for a path leading off right through the wood to open fields. Cross into the field and continue ahead over the fields to the road, your exit being marked by a signpost.

3. Cross directly over with care and walk down the back lane towards Newton on the Hill, where Richard Gough, social historian was born. He prepared a fascinating history of Myddle at the turn of the 18th century using the church congregation as a reference. It provides an interesting social comment. Mr Gough, despite being criticised for his work, given its uncomplimentary nature in places, lived to a ripe old age of 88. The air must be good at Newton on the Hill.

4. Go through the hamlet and by the last house on the right there's a stile just beyond the drive. Cross it and go ahead to a stile by a water tank. Climb over and walk ahead again to exit onto a busy road, so be alert. Cross the road and turn left. Go left to walk past the forge and then go right to walk alongside a wall, then along the field's edge to the corner and then right along the wood's edge. Cross a stile and keep left to follow the edge and to the left of the water tank. Cross a stile by the gate and keep ahead on the woodland path and as this bends right go left over a stile. At the junction by the entrance to the quarry go left.

5. At the road go left and pass by beautiful cottages, which look as if they are out of a fairy tale, en route to Webscott. Turn right at the junction, signposted to Bomere Heath, passing by a private garage, which was once a Primitive Methodist Chapel, erected in 1842. Take the next turning right up to the Webscott Farm.

6. The concrete track proceeds ahead to pass by the barns into a yard but bear left through a barred gate, well before reaching the farmhouse. This track runs ahead mainly through dairy pastures and a small wood. You'll notice a bridle gate on the right. Go through here and continue ahead to the next gate and ahead once again along the hedge at first but then across the field at the end to another gate, which leads out onto an old track near to Hollins Farm.

7. Turn right and follow this splendid old track, which can get very muddy at times, towards Myddle. After nearly a mile, and as the lane bends right sharply, go over the little footbridge and stile on the right, turn left and head for the houses on the edge of the village. You come to a bridle gate (look for the signpost) on your left onto the road. Turn right to walk back into the village by the ancient church and near the castle site. It is time to reflect on what Gough actually meant in that intriguing early work.

The parish church, Myddle

25. Nesscliffe

Moderate walking as there are some climbs. On a clear day the views from Cliffe Common are admirable. The highpoint is the rich sandstone edges leading to Kynaston's Cave on the last leg of the walk.

Distance	6 miles (10km)
Allow	3 hours
Map	OS Explorer 240 Oswestry
By bus	There is a frequent bus service 70 between Shrewsbury and Oswestry which runs Mondays to Saturdays and a two hourly frequency on Sundays. Ask for the Old Three Pidgeons public house
By car	Nesscliffe is situated just off the A5. There is car parking at Nesscliffe Hill Country Park
Refreshments	There are refreshments at The Old Three Pigeons and also at the Talbot Inn and Top House Inn at Ruyton-XI-Towns
Nearest Tourist Information Office	Rowley's House, Barker Street Tel: 01743 281200

Nesscliffe is a small village mid-way between Shrewsbury and Oswestry with its own garage, hotel and public house. It has become more popular in recent years as Shropshire Council has established a country park here including access to Kynaston Cave where a notorious outlaw lived with his faithful horse, Beelzebub. He has gained his place in the local history books as a 'rob the rich to give to the poor' type of villain.

Ruyton-XI-Towns is a large village which once had Borough status. It was endowed in the 14th century and included eleven manorial locations and hence the name. It is unusual, if not unique, in having Roman numerals included in its title. The local heritage group is seeking to conserve the very best of the village including the castle overlooking the

River Perry and the church, both of which date originally from the 13th century. There are two pubs to hand, The Talbot and Top House Inn as well as a shop.

1. Start the walk from the Old Three Pidgeons Inn in Nesscliffe (as the bus stops here). Cross the main road to walk along a lane signposted to Valeswood. In twenty steps or so, go right through a kissing gate and enter the country park. Rise to the junction and turn left, as signposted to Oliver's Point. Keep ahead at the first junction and at the next go left to Oaks Car Park. On reaching the road look for a stile almost opposite.

2. Cross the stile and head slightly right across the field. Look for the stile next to the double barred gate. Climb over and turn right up to a junction at the road in Hopton. Turn left and pass by a large farm. The lane descends a little to the turning to Startewood. Enter the drive but then cross the stile on the left. Head slightly left, i.e. follow the direction of the three stiles in a succession of fields. You reach a field corner by two oak trees. Your way is slightly left again towards another large tree. Cross the stiles and footbridge at this point.

3. Go right to cross a footbridge on the right and pass by a pool as you make your way through a small thicket to another stile. You now enter a large field where you follow the field's edge ahead with a hedge to your right. This leads to a lovely old track and you soon pass through a gate and by a dwelling. Keep ahead and this becomes Pound Lane which is wider and less green to arrive at Ruyton-XI-Towns.

4. If you are stopping awhile keep ahead to the main road. Otherwise, go right at the first junction, to walk up a lane known as Big Walls. They are indeed lovely sandstone retaining walls. Ignore Startlewood Lane on the right and instead go to the next turning, Little Ness Road, where you turn right. You reach a walled garden and house on the left. At this point leave the road to walk up (right) to a small settlement known as The Cliffe.

5. Take the left fork to climb up the hillside and at the top of the bank go right. You rise up to a viewpoint and seat. Carved initials of lovers are there for all to see in the soft red sandstone rock. It begs the question as to how many are still together. Look at that view. There's

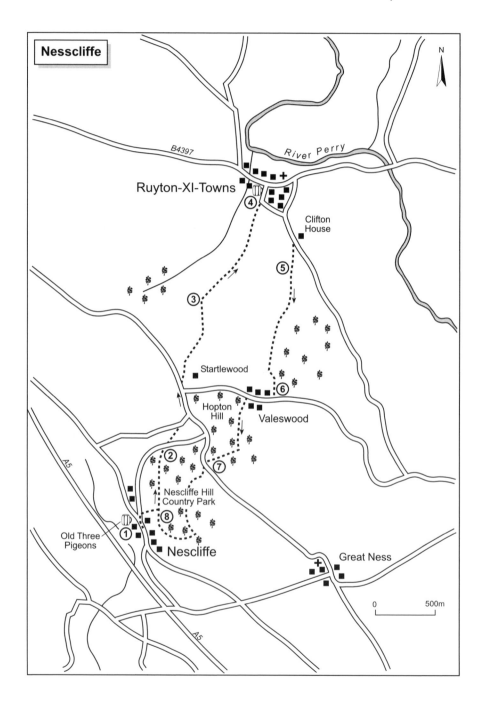

a seascape of rapeseed rolling in the summer breeze. One of Shropshire's very own oil producer crushes these local crops at nearby Great Ness; not many food miles there then. The oil that is good for you too. To the west, there are the gently wooded hillocks looking towards Oswestry and the Welsh mountains beyond. Draw yourself away and walk on to a crossroads. Go ahead and pass through woods. Ignore the path to the right, keeping left and climbing still. Then, go left to descend at the bottom and turn right along a track to a lane.

6. Go right at the lane. Ignore the first turning to the left but as the road begins to descend go left into woodland The path passes a dwelling; ignore turnings to the left. Keep ahead through tall trees, your track soon bends to the right. You reach a lane. Cross this.

7. Go through a kissing gate and across a small pasture to enter the wood. Keep left to pass by a farm to a junction where you turn right. Follow this track through the wood as signposted to Kynaston's Cave. On reaching the pool turn right again. Not far beyond cut right again and go ahead at the next junction by fencing. Take real care here, for you need to walk down a series of steps overlooking a considerable drop to the floor of these old workings. There's something rather magical about it all; woodland cover, sandstone cliffs and then to come across Kynaston's cave. This is the place. This is where at least one local rogue hid successfully from the sheriff's men and then legend has it he was pardoned. There's no access to the cave but the thought of living with a horse in a confined space plays on my mind.

8. From the cave entrance go left down more steps to re-join a main path. Turn right and then left to regain your path back to The Old Three Pidgeons. What a walk. There are so many landscape types within such proximity. It must be time for a beer.

26. Oswestry

This walk offers a mixture of scenery from gentle pasture and parkland to thickly wooded slopes. A marvellous walk which includes a few steep climbs and more excellent views.

Distance	7 miles (11km)
Allow	3-4 hours
Map	OS Explorer 240 Oswestry
By bus	There is a regular service from Shrewsbury and Wrexham
By car	Oswestry is signposted from the A5 by-pass of the town. There are several car parks near to the centre but these are very congested on market day, Wednesday
Refreshments	Plentiful supply in Oswestry
Nearest Tourist Information Office	Heritage Centre, Oswestry Tel: 01691 662753

Oswestry is very much the border market town, being the host of Shropshire's largest street market every Wednesday. It is steeped in history from early times to the industrial era. The Iron Age hill fort on the outskirts of town is very visible and commanding although not on high ground. Oswestry was also the site of a Marcher Lords castle, along with Whittington and Chirk.

For railway lovers the station and old workshops area of the town are a sad reflection of the former Cambrian Railway headquarters. Hopefully, the Cambrian Railways Society and Cambrian Railways Trust will be able to re-establish a passenger link to Gobowen in years to come. It will be a welcome addition to existing attractions.

1. Start from outside St Oswald's church in Church Street. Go left through the recreational ground to join Brynhafod Road. Walk up this road and as it bends right into Hampton Road go ahead on a lovely old bridleway. Three cheers for the local residents or planners who managed to keep this from the encroachment or urbanisation that surrounds it. The bridleway continues ahead; it is sometimes wet and in parts a little on the smelly side. Plough on! It finally gives out at a gate into a field where you'll see High Fawr Farm ahead.

2. Go right to climb a stile and keep ahead to a corner, where you keep left to follow the field hedge on your right, up to another corner. Cross a stile and then go ahead to a stile of sorts by a barred gate. Cross this and go immediately left through a barred gate. Now proceed right to follow the hedge on your right, again up to a stile. Climb this and head slightly left over a field to cross a stile by a water tank, where you go left to a barred gate in the next field. One through, head diagonally across the field towards a large house. You meet with electric telegraph poles as you near the garden wall. Follow the wall to the corner and cut slightly left to a barred gate in the corner.

3. Go through the gate onto the road and cross the road to walk down Bwlch Lane. This bends right and then continues up the hill to Bwlch. At the corner, cross a stile into a yard and another by a barn. Walk ahead with the hedge on the left and cross two more stiles. Keep ahead alongside a wood but look for a stile on the left into the forest. There's light at the end of the tunnel as you soon reach Offa's Dyke National Trail.

4. Go left on Offa's Dyke Path in Racecourse Wood and continue ahead through beautiful woods on this Welsh borderland escarpment. The path drops a little and curves right to cross a boundary fence then left. It now follows a steady contour for a while before beginning to descend once again, through scrub and curving round an outcrop of rock. What a fortification Offa's Dyke must have been, using the natural advantage of the land on its 142-mile divide between Wales and Mercia.

5. At the T-junction of paths, go right then next left, following the signs to a path which now falls more sharply to another junction. Go left and downwards, rather than immediately left. Continue ahead, passing

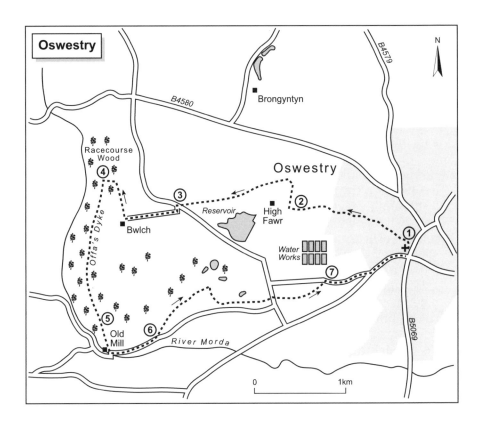

by a cottage and along a lane to a road.

Go left up the hill and as the wood begins to open up you will see an entrance drive to your left. Turn immediately right along a narrow path.

6. Cross a stile and go slightly left upwards to another stile. Go over this and continue ahead in a slightly left direction through exquisite parkland to meet a green track which is just discernible, coming from the cottage seen on your left. Head for the barred gate and walls where there's a stile to cross. There are the remains of a walled garden to the left. Follow the path which enters the wood by a stile and follow the path, which curves right to a marker. Go right and come to a stile by a gate. Keep ahead on a green track down the field. This curves left down to a lane. Cross over and the path keeps ahead at first then curves left

to pass beneath hawthorns to your left. Cross a stile and head slightly right to a field corner by a house. Exit on to the road.

7. Go right down Broomhall Lane and come to the main road. Turn left back into town where you cut left into the churchyard of St Oswald's.

27. Pontesbury

Easy walking along paths with a few climbs. An opportunity to visit Poles Coppice and Earl's Hill Nature reserve.

Distance	**5 miles (8km)**
Allow	**3 hours**
Map	**OS Explorers 216 Welshpool and Montgomery, 241 Shrewsbury**
By bus	**There is a regular daily service from Shrewsbury (Barker Street bus station). There is a bus stop just before the Red Lion at Chapel Street. The Shropshire Hills Shuttle also serves Pontesbury and Habberley on summer weekends**
By car	**Follow the A488 from Shrewsbury to Pontesbury. The road splits in the village and there is a limited amount of on-street parking**
Refreshments	**Pontesbury has three public houses and shops. There is also The Mytton Arms at Habberley, which should definitely be on you list to visit**
Nearest Tourist Information Office	**Rowley's House, Barker Street Tel: 01743 281200**

St George's church dominates this now mainly dormitory village lying between Shrewsbury and Bishop's Castle. Dating from Norman times, but mainly restored in the nineteenth century, it is a landmark for miles around. So are Pontesford and Earl's hills, the latter having been dedicated as a nature reserve. Pontesbury was once the home of Mary Webb, famous Shropshire novelist who is currently enjoying increased popularity.

Pontesbury has been the gateway for much quarrying in the area and at one time there was a railway to Minsterley, principally for the large creamery, but also for passengers. There were exchange sidings at Pontesbury for the Snailbeach mines as the tramway was of a different gauge. The aim is to reopen the old lines for walking and cycling.

1. Start the walk from The Red Lion public house in Pontesbury. Walk on the road towards the church and opposite turn left on a road signposted for Pontesbury Hill. This bends to the left and then right. Climb up the bank but look out for a path between gardens on the left. Go through the kissing gate and a small gate and ahead to another two kissing gates in succession to reach a track.

2. Go right and follow this past a dwelling and it then bends slightly right towards a cottage. Before the next barred gate go right over a stile in the corner. Go left up the pasture and cross another stile. Then go almost immediately left along a green path between the cottage and garden.

3. Keep ahead on a well warn track through the wood which soon curves right to pass   dwellings. Go left through the bridle gate here, signposted to Poles Coppice. This bends to the right with a group of buildings and farm. Keep to the lower path and perimeter fence to the next stile. Cross it and go right to the next gate. Once through go left and walk through wet ground in Lees Coppice. Follow the path as it winds its way through the wood and with deviations to avoid the wetter ground. Persevere for the path rises slightly away from the water-logged surface. It bends right (ignore the path down to gate on left) and you reach a junction. Go left here through a barred gate into the pasture.

4. Keep ahead along the hedge and fence on your left. This curves around to a barred gate in the field corner. Go through into the next field still with the hedge to your left. You reach a track which runs by large barns and buildings to the road in Habberley. Go left and at the junction turn right signposted for Pulverbatch. At the next junction go left to pass the church and arrive at The Mytton Arms (which happens to be the stop for the Shropshire Hills Shuttles).

5. Keep ahead to follow the road around the corner. But then go left over a stile and walk between gardens to another stile. Walk across the field

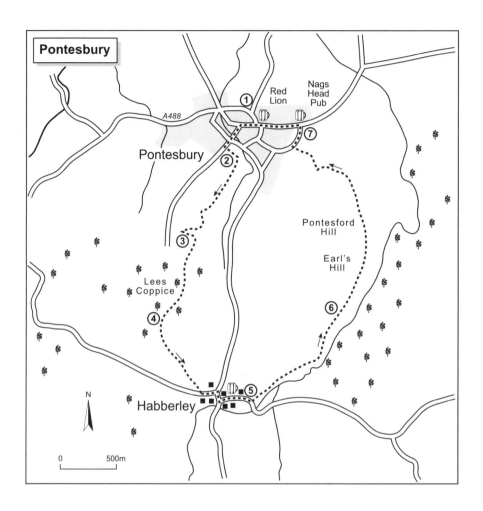

slightly right until you come to the next stile and into woodland. Go
left to rise through the woodland to a stile on the left, which leads into
a track. This gives out into a field and you keep ahead alongside the
hedge on the left. Proceed through the gateway and in the next field
aim slightly left to climb up to the top left corner to a small gate.

6. This is Earl's Hill Nature Reserve. You join a path coming in from the
   left. Go right here and walk over scree and beneath woodland to Ant
   Hill Meadow, home to the rarer yellow meadow ant. Keep ahead to

cross the stile and then slightly right to re-join woodland. Follow the track as it bends left to Pontesford Hill car park. Drop down to the lane. Go right and then first left on a track leading to houses. This bends to the right into a field which is now on your left. Head slightly right, across the field, to a stile in the far corner. Go right and come to a junction by the school. Go right here to exit by The Nag's Head public house. There's a bus top for Shrewsbury here. Otherwise, turn left for the short walk back to the Red Lion.

28. Prees to Wem

Easy walking through a gentle landscape; the main feature is Edstaston church with its fine Norman architecture. This is a linear walk between Prees and Wem railway stations.

Distance	5 miles (8km)
Allow	2-3 hours
Map	OS Explorer 241 Shrewsbury
By train	Preferably, travel to Prees by train. There is a reasonably good daily service, approximately two hourly, between Crewe and Shrewsbury which stops at Prees (but the Sunday service is a little less frequent). Prees is a request stop so you have to tell the conductor guard that you want that stop! There are more return trains from Wem
By bus	The 511 regular bus service links Shrewsbury, Wem and Prees on Mondays to Saturdays
By car	Travel on the A49 between Whitchurch and Shrewsbury and then the B5063 to Wem
Refreshments	Wem has a number of public houses, a café and at least one fish and chip shop
Nearest Tourist Information Office	Rowley's House, Barker Street Tel: 01743 281200

Wem lies in the southern quarter of Shropshire's major cheese producing area. Its fortunes were not wholly based on cheese however, as it also had millers, tanners and a brewery trade. The latter closed and many a drinker curses the owners, Greenall Whitley, for this deed. Wem is also a market town and a small number of traditional shops have survived in the High Street. It enjoys a Sweet Pea festival in order to celebrate one time local resident, Henry Eckford, who developed the sweet pea as a scented blossom.

This is a linear walk, i.e. not a circular. If you are travelling by car the suggestion is to park near to Wem station, catch the train to Prees and walk back to Wem. Prees is a request stop so tell the conductor guard that you would like to alight there. It has to be the loneliest station on the line between Crewe and Shrewsbury, for there is only a farm nearby and the signalbox. The large village of Prees is a good mile away.

1. From the railway station platform (where trains for Crewe depart) cross the road and walk along the track with the signal box to your left. The track soon curves to the right and at this point you bear left on a bridleway between the trees towards the railway line. Follow the boundary fence to mid field then strike off right. Head for the gate and over the stream. In the next field, head slightly right to join the remnants of a hedge. Follow this ahead to a gateway in the top corner of the field.

2. Go right to walk facing the traffic on the road until it reaches a farm and junction at Pepperstreet. Cross before reaching this point. Turn left and follow the quieter lane which passes Edstaston Hall to the B5476. This is far busier. Cross with care and turn left to walk along the verge past the houses for about 100 metres or so to a stile on the right. Cross it and enter a field. Keep ahead with the stream to your right until you reach the remains of a wooden fence. At this point, head towards Edstaston church, which has several interesting Norman features and is well worth a visit. Just to the right of the churchyard is a stile where you enter the outer graveyard. Go over it and through a small gate then ahead to a bridle gate onto the road.

3. To the right you should see the old line of the Prees branch of the Shropshire Union Canal abandoned in the 1800s. Several sections are in water so as to attract wildlife and are managed by the Shropshire Wildlife Trust. Go left on the road and at the corner by the church cross over to cross a stile and walk down a drive. Climb a second stile to enter a field. Keep ahead to reach a stile by a barred gate. Climb this and now head slightly right but keeping to the left of a pool. Cross a

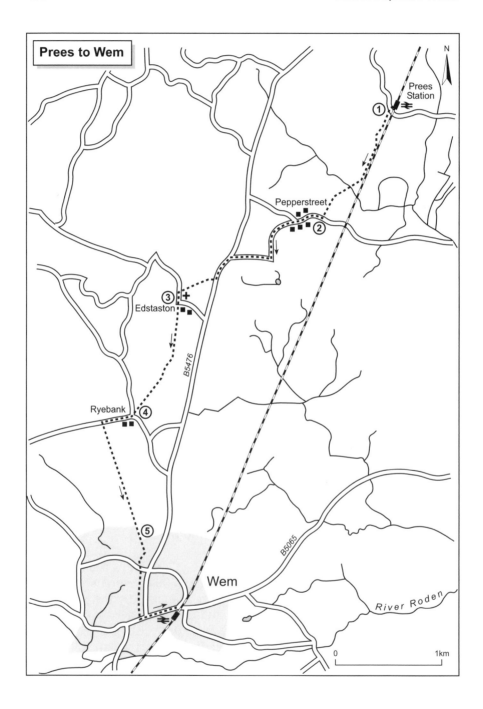

stile and follow the field's edge on the left to a stile beneath trees. Go across the next field to a stile adjacent to a barred gate. Keeping ahead and aim for a white house in the distance. Cross the stile and keep ahead to another by a barred gate. This leads onto a road.

4. Turn left and then right, as signposted to Loppington. Pass by a farm and a pool. Then, go left over a stile into a pasture. Follow this ahead in a succession of fields on a well walked path. You will see Wem church in the distance and the spire of Clive church in the far distance. You eventually come to a footbridge, which you cross and proceed ahead to a stile. Go over it and keep ahead for 100 metres to cross a stile on the right. Go left to follow the hedge on your left and go through a small gate to follow the corralled path to the edge of town.

5. This leads to a metalled path between gardens and into Barnfield. Cut immediately left through to Marcroft which you follow around to a junction. Go left to the main road. Cross here and walk down an old town path, by the industrial estate and to the High Street. Turn left for the railway station passing by the pleasant Millennium Green where you can rest awhile if the mood takes you.

29. Pulverbatch

A moderately hard walk in that it involves many climbs up to the Thresholds Centre; from there the walking is easier. Excellent views are a bonus and there's the Jug and Bottle as a mid-way stop.

Distance	9 miles (15 km)
Allow	5 hours
Map	OS Explorer 217 The Long Mynd and Wenlock Edge
By bus	There is an hourly bus from Shrewsbury on Mondays to Saturdays. The Shropshire Hills shuttles serve Pulverbatch
By car	In Shrewsbury, travel on the B4380 (Roman Road) from Meole Brace to the roundabout by the cemetery. Go left into Longden Road for Pulverbatch. There is limited on street parking in the village
Refreshments	The White Horse Inn at Pulverbatch and the Jug and Bottle at Picklescott, which is an absolute must
Nearest Tourist Information Office	Rowley's House, Barker Street Tel: 01743 281200

Pulverbatch is situated on the old road to Bishop's Castle on the very edge of the Shropshire Hills Area of Outstanding Natural Beauty. There is an unusual castle located in the village with an inner and outer bailey. The area is known as The Knapp. For centuries most people hereabout were engaged in local agriculture but in recent decades the village has become more dormitory. The White Horse pub, a 15th century building, is one of the focal points of the village and this is where the Shropshire Shuttles bus and Shrewsbury bus calls. It is an ideal starting point for this ramble. Picklescott is a quieter location where a group of houses nestle around the crossroads and stream. The Bottle and Glass is one of the oldest buildings;

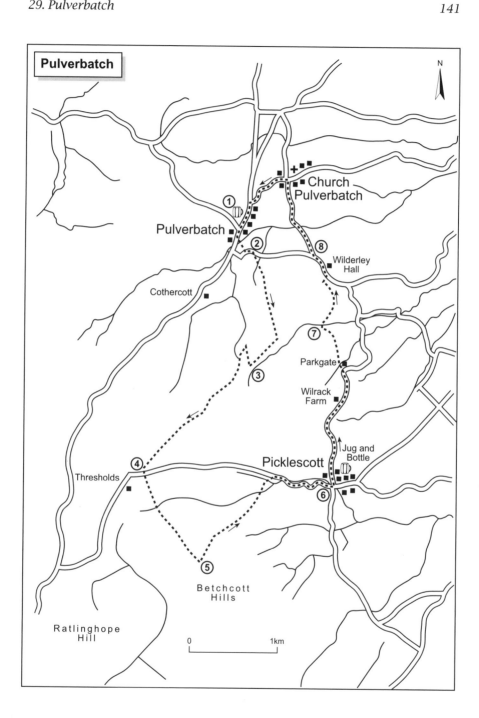

it dates from the 16th Century but like the White Horse, it became a pub sometime in the 19th century. It is a wonderful rural survivor.

1. Start from the White Horse Inn at Pulverbatch. Cross the road in front of the pub but be on the look out for cars as visibility is poor. Go right and walk down the hill. At the bottom of the hill you cross a stile on the left. Then, go ahead, cross a footbridge and another stile. In the next field, head slightly right to climb steps and a stile onto a road. Go left here.

2. Before the farm on the left go right through a gateway into a large field. Head for the two oaks mid-field and then walk up and ahead to cross a stile by a barred gate. Now go slightly left across a field with great views of the Stiperstones and The Wrekin. Go through the barred gate and ahead to the next boundary where you'll find a double stile and plank bridge across a ditch. Head slightly right across the next field to the far hedge and turn right to walk up the field to pass Beeches Farm.

3. Cross a stile by the gate, go over the track and pass through a gate into another pasture. Keep ahead on a green way. This curves to the right and the right of way actually cuts right to a hawthorn hedge and then left to the stile you can see by the gate. The right of way is ahead. It is almost in a parallel line to the hedge on the right but therein lies a problem, for this is real wetland and thus the path weaves its way between springs and marsh; it is a deliciously squelchy experience not to be missed. Cross a stile by a gate (ignore the one to the right) and keep ahead alongside the wood. At the top strike off slightly right over an expansive field to a double stile and then head in a similar direction, but keeping to the left of a boundary marker post.

4. On the road, turn right for the Thresholds Centre, about a five minute walk, where there are displays about local culture and landscape. The Centre is featured in Alistair Sawday's book *Go Slow in England*. If you are not calling then cross the road and proceed along The Portway, an ancient road dating from Roman times. You reach a point where there's a barred gate ahead and the Shropshire Way peels off to the right.

5. You go left through a bridle gate and head slightly left to follow the fencing to a gate which stands to the left of three trees. Go through it

and walk ahead down the field where you'll find a track that passes a house. Keep ahead down the track until you reach a lane. Go right here for Picklescott, where you go left for the Bottle and Glass pub.

6. If you are not stopping then walk past the entrance to the pub and leave the village on a back road to Wilderley Hall. Pass Wildrack Farm and then descend to a group of dwellings, Parkgate, where you go left down a tractor track, sometimes waterlogged, and to a field. As the track bears left you go ahead down along the hedge to cross the stile into the wood. The path drops more steeply to a plank bridge and then becomes less clear. Your way is slightly left up the hillside to hit a track. Go left and then next right as way-marked.

7. Cross a stile to exit the wood and turn right. Go over the next stile and now head slightly left and through a gap by a water tank. Head for a point just to the left of the farm complex. There's a circular motte castle mound to the left but it is difficult to see from here; you'll have to use your imagination at this point. Join a track and go right to walk down to junction. Turn left to walk through the farm and keep ahead on the lane. Continue down the hill to a corner where you go right on a bridleway to Church Pulverbatch.

8. This lovely old lane, festooned with bluebells and blossom, runs down to cross a stream and then climbs into the village of Church Pulverbatch, known in past times as Churton, which is a shortened version of Church Town. The beautiful church stands near to Churton Farm. When the bridleway reaches the road go left for Pulverbatch and it is a ten minute walk back to The White Horse

30. Richard's Castle to Ludlow

The main features of the walk are Richard's Castle and church as well as the magnificent views from Mortimer Forest

Distance	7-8 miles (12km)
Allow	4-5 hours
Map	OS Explorer 203 Ludlow and Cleobury Mortimer
By train	Ludlow is well-served by daily trains from Shrewsbury and Hereford
By bus	There is a daily bus from Birmingham/ Kidderminster and Hereford to Ludlow. The 492 bus calls at Richards Castle. Ask the driver for Richard's Castle. The bus stops by the Castle Inn
By car	From the A49 from Shrewsbury to Hereford there are signs to the Park and Ride service for Ludlow which operates every 15 minutes until just after 6 pm. This avoids bringing congestion in Ludlow itself
Refreshments	There are several public houses and cafés at Ludlow and the Castle Inn at Richard's Castle, although it is only open Sunday lunchtimes and otherwise in the evening from 7 pm onwards
Nearest Tourist Information Office	Castle Street, Ludlow Tel: 01584 875053

Despite the slow encroachment of supermarkets and car parks, Ludlow remains an enchanting town (see Chapter 20 for a little more detail). This is a linear ramble which follows Mortimer Trail from The Goggin to

Ludlow through Mortimer's Forest. The outing starts at Ludlow Assembly Rooms where you catch the 492 bus for the 10 minute ride to Richard's Castle. It's a lovely walk up to The Goggin and along the Mortimer Trail up to High Vinnals and through the forest back to Ludlow.

Richard's Castle, as its name suggests, was a Norman stronghold. The scant remains of the fortifications stand near to the church at the top end of the village. The views from this vantage point over to the Malvern hills are worth the climb up from the Castle Inn.

High Vinnals, the highest ground in Mortimer Forest, offers exceptional views across Shropshire and Herefordshire.

1. Alight from the bus at The Castle pub at Richard's Castle. Go up the lane by the pub passing by a fine set of half timbered buildings such as Court House with its fine dovecote. It is about half a mile to the cross roads where you keep ahead for a steeper climb up to the church and castle ruins. Pass by Green Farm and then the road curves right by a small green.

2. At this point go left along a track to pass by the entrance to the church; it is well worth a visit. Otherwise, go through the gate and walk slightly right along a greenway to another gate located to the right of the barns. Once through the gate, go right on a more prominent track which runs beneath the wooded castle mound and crosses a stream. Rise up the valley by a small plantation to a gate and then continue ahead to Goggin Copse on the left.

3. At The Goggin, you'll need to pause a moment to catch your breath. Take a look back over to The Malverns, Clee Hill and other lesser hills in Herefordshire. The Goggin is actually in Herefordshire and is a rather special place, wrapped in the warmth of the borderland; the pace of change has been slow here. The name is special too. Its derivation and meaning is uncertain. Once through the gate keep ahead with the hedge to your right.

4. Go through a barred gate to join The Mortimer Trail, an understated walking route that links Ludlow and Kington, as initially developed in 1996. It follows a succession of ridges through some very quiet country rich in wildlife and with link routes down to the villages for an overnight stop. So, go right and the enclosed track leads to a wide expanse known as Hanway Common. Aim slightly left here to meet

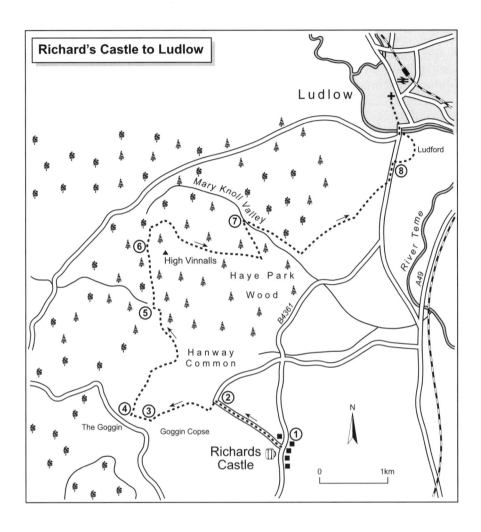

with the hedgerow on the left and follow this along the common, past an entrance and then by a seat kindly supplied for the weary walker.

5. The path comes to a small gate in the top left corner and you now enter Mortimer Forest. Do not be put off by the first very muddy section. Keep ahead as the Herefordshire Trail peels left. On reaching the barrier and a wider track go right and immediately left on the

forestry track. This can get a little on the dusty side in dry weather but the reason for the route soon becomes apparent. Ease up to take in the view of the exquisite ridges across to The Radnor Forest and into Mid Wales.

6. This is the landmark of High Vinnals and you will now begin to descend. Keep right at the junction and the track runs ahead. Ignore the turning to the left and at the next junction keep ahead descending gently for most of the time, a pleasant experience after the climb up to Vinnals. Follow the Mortimer Trail signs as the green path runs ahead and then cuts left on a lesser path down to the valley bottom. Go left and then right to follow it up to a cottage known as Sunnydingle. Here you join a track. The track rises up to a sharp bend but you go ahead through a gate and along a bridle way. This runs through to a building, Starvecrow, and continues ahead over a stile by a gate to descend to meet a more prominent track. Go left. Follow this to a field. Keep ahead to reach a stile. Cross this and walk ahead along the edge of a garden and along a drive to exit on the main road. Go left for the last section into Ludlow, unfortunately along a pavement.

Autumnal mist at Richard's Castle

View from High Vinnals

Before the main road descends, go right to cross the road and walk along a cul de sac. At the barred gate, go left to walk alongside the field to Ludford. Keep ahead by the memorial garden and splendid houses to the main road again by the entrance to Ludford Church. Go right to pass by the Charlton Arms (walkers are welcome in the bar). Cross the Ludford bridge into Ludlow and keep ahead through the old gateway up Broad Street and left for the Market Square and castle.

7. This walk ends at the magnificent castle, standing at the head of Castle Square and above the fast flowing waters of the River Teme. The castle most probably dates from the 11th century and the main fortifications were added during the 12th and 13th centuries. The castle was held by the de Lacy family and then the de Genevilles before becoming a Mortimer fortress. It was held by Royalist supporters in the English Civil War and suffered much damage at this time. Between then and the early 19th century it fell into disrepair. Since 1811 it has been in the hands of the Earls of Powys and is open to the public and hosts many festivals and events.

31. Shrewsbury

Easy walking from the very centre of Shrewsbury to Haughmond Abbey by way of the Shrewsbury canal. This is a loop walk but you can catch the bus out and walk back. The full walk is not possible when the Severn is in flood.

Distance	7 miles (12km)
Allow	4 hours
Map	OS Explorer 241 Shrewsbury
By train	This is the hub of the border railway network with direct services from Cardiff, Chester, London, Manchester and The Midlands
By bus	If you wish to travel out to Haughmond Abbey and walk back then catch the 519 Newport bus which is two hourly Mondays to Saturdays
By car	Shrewsbury is also at the crossroads of major roads A5 and A49. Best to use one of the park and ride services as congestion and parking in Shrewsbury makes this a far better option
Refreshments	Plentiful supply in Shrewsbury and The Corbet Arms in Uffington
Nearest Tourist Information Office	Rowley's House, Barker Street Tel: 01743 281200

Shrewsbury Railway station is one of the finest examples of Victorian railway architecture in the region; it was built in the 1840s using stone from Grinshill (see walk 36).

From 1862 the station was under the stewardship of two great rivals, the Great Western Railway and the London North Western Railway company (the latter became the London, Midland and Scottish Railway). It was, by all accounts, a substantial enterprise in the town with over 500 employees based at the station alone, plus others at the engine sheds and other locations. The station still retains an air of business as it has a considerable number of arrivals per day and there's still even a degree of rivalry between companies plying for London traffic.

Even if you have an hour between trains it is possible to walk awhile. The core of this beautiful town still retains its medieval layout with an overlay of half timbered and Tudor buildings. Walk to point 2 and then turn right to follow the riverside path through Quarry Gardens back to Victoria Avenue and the busy Smithfield Road.

Haughmond Abbey was established in the early decades of the 12th century and was ransacked in 1539 during the Dissolution of the Monastries commanded by Henry VIII. The chapter room is the best preserved section of the abbey including tombstones of saints. Haughmond Hill is a favourite location of Shrewsbury countrygoers; it is managed by Forest Enterprise and encourages bikers and dog walkers.

1. Start the walks from the entrance to the railway station. Walk up to the concourse main road but go immediately left here to pass by a shop and to steps before reaching Platform 3. The sandstone walls of Shrewsbury Castle stand to your right. Walk up the steps to the overbridge and this leads to The Dana where Shrewsbury Gaol is located. The original building dates from the late 18th century. Note the bust of Howard noted for his work on penal reform in the 19th century. The last person to be hanged at Shrewsbury Gaol was John Mapp in 1868, following his conviction for murder. It attracted many thousands of people standing at this very place. Go right along the Dana and as the road bends left go ahead, down steps to the riverside.

2. Go left along the riverside walk. You share it with cyclists so be aware of this. It has a surprisingly rural feel given the gardens and greenery. Continue along Sydney Avenue and you need to follow this into Darville, the boring bit (as the path alongside the river has collapsed at this point). Look for the Severn Way signs to guide you right and through a modern estate; walk through it. Look for the signs on the right, which indicates your way on a route between gardens.

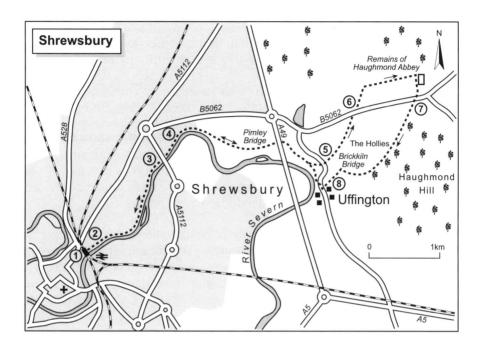

3. Before reaching the tunnel beneath the inner ring road, go right back towards the river and leave the Severn Way (the steps up to the bridge) as you proceed towards the river and then left to go under the bridge. Cross two streams and on reaching the fork, go left to rise up to join the Shropshire Way on a multi-user path.

4. Go right to follow the track through to Uffington by the remnants of the Shrewsbury and Newport Canal. It was built in the 1790s to transport coal from the Telford area to Shrewsbury. It is still in water in some parts and offers an opportunity to see moorhens and ducks enjoying the greener habitats. You will come to a road at Pimley Manor. Cross this and continue ahead beneath the outer by-pass. Ignore the stile and continue to the road at the edge of Uffington.

5. Cross the road and look for the footpath signposted to Haughmond Hill. Walk along this track and proceed through a kissing gate by a barred gate. Within 20 paces cut left along a path which passes a pumping station to enter a field. Keep ahead along the hedge, ignoring

a path which peels off across the field. Go through a kissing gate and onward to a corner where you'll find another kissing gate. Once through, turn left and walk to a stile leading onto the main road.

6. Go over the road with care and cross a stile to walk through a pasture. Cross another stile and go right. Walk towards Haughmond Abbey through a succession of fields passing near to Hillside and Abbey Farms. You reach a stile by the ruins. Go right over this and walk along the perimeter to another stile and then left to the entrance to the abbey. It is open daily in the main season and there is a charge. If not visiting, go right along the entrance track to the main road. Cross again with care and enter the woodland known as The Hollies.

7. The path runs ahead and there have been some deviations made by people meandering a little. However, on reaching the major junction go right and follow the track to a point where there are electricity pylons. Just before go left to a stile which you cross. Proceed ahead and you pass over a canal bridge. The Shrewsbury Canal is in water

The serene ruins of Haughmond Abbey

here. Keep ahead again to cross a stile by dwellings and down to the main road in Uffington and The Corbet Arms.

8. Go right at the Corbet Arms to walk through the village and turn left down a track at the corner to a field. Go ahead through the riverside meadow to a stile and re-join the track used on the outward leg. Retrace your steps back into Shrewsbury.

32. Stiperstones

This is a strenuous walk as the first climb up Mytton Dingle is steep and offers a challenge. The reward is a magnificent view over to Wales and a walk which dips into an area of industrial heritage near Snailbeach.

Distance	**4 miles (6-7km)**
Allow	**2½ hours**
Map	**OS Explorer 216 Welshpool and Montgomery**
By bus	**There is a service from Shrewsbury to Stiperstones on Mondays to Saturdays. The village is served by the Shropshire Shuttle service on weekends between April and the end of October**
By car	**Travel on the A488 road to Plox Green. Turn left to Stiperstones and The Bog where you turn left for the road to Cranberry Rocks car park. Alternatively, choose the back road to Bishop's Castle, off the A5, through Pulverbatch to Bridges where you turn right**
Refreshments	**The Stiperstones Inn and shop at Stiperstones are well worth the visit**
Nearest Tourist Information Office	**Rowley's House, Barker Street Tel: 01743 281200**

Mysterious they look and mysterious they are, for the Stiperstones is an area rich in folklore and superstition depicted in Mary Webb's novel *Gone to Earth*. More importantly, the area is a National Nature Reserve as it is of biological and geological interest. As with other Shropshire upland areas it is covered in heather, bracken and gorse with bilberries, and cowberries in places. The views are magnificent. It is hard to believe that the area has also been subject to considerable mining activity especially in the Snailbeach area, where lead ore was mined extensively as well as zinc, barites and other minerals. The Snailbeach mine, which closed in 1955, is open to the public on Sundays between Easter and the end of October. It is managed by the Shropshire Mines Trust Ltd. Google Snailbeach Mine for details.

1. Start from the Stiperstones Inn. Go right and right again. Then choose the left hand fork signposted to Mytton Dingle. This climbs up by houses and through a yard to a stile by a gate. Cross this and walk ahead. Before the entrance to cottages the bridleway eases away to the left to enter the Stiperstones Nature Reserve. Now, the path really does climb into the hillside. It is a steep, hard climb towards the top, so make sure you take it at a pace to suit your stamina.

2. Breathe a sigh of relief at the top and take time to admire the view across to Wales. The path continues ahead on a green swathe and a wider track joins from the right. Keep ahead again. However, before reaching the barred gate in the distance look for a little path which cuts off to the left (there's a small pile of stones acting as a marker here).

3. This path soon joins a fence on your right. Proceed ahead to cross a stile by a gate and keep near to the fence again as it bends left. You will see Crow's Nest Gully below but your way is to follow the perimeter fence on the right to cross another stile. Go through a kissing gate on the right and keep ahead (ignoring the stile to the left). Pass through a gate and stile and continue to follow the fence down to a gate, where you cross your next stile. Walk down the track by a line of hawthorns to a gate before Lordshill Farm. Go left here to cross two stiles and to skirt to the left of a barn. Then go right to cross another stile on to a drive where you turn left. Follow this down to a junction.

4. If you turn left you can walk to the Snailbeach mine (about 10 minutes walk). Otherwise, go right to pass a cottage and Lordshill Chapel. The chapel was originally built in 1833 but the one you see now dates from the 1870s. This romantic setting was captured by Mary Webb in her book *Gone to Earth*, which was published in 1917 and was also used in the film of the book released in the 1950s.

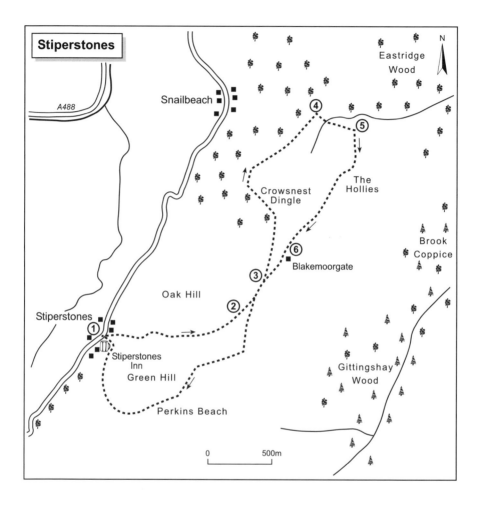

5. Keep ahead on the bridleway as it climbs the hillside and at the fork take the higher track through the Hollies, a holly wood that is being restored by the Shropshire Wildlife Trust. The track curves to the right, leading to a barred gate. Keep ahead and with the fence to your right as you proceed to a line of conifers across the landscape. Cross the stile by the gate and head diagonally across the field to the far corner where there is another stile by a gate. Cross it and walk up the green track to another stile. Once over go right.

6. Follow the main track as it rises across the heathland. Before reaching the summit there is a tractor track to the right which cuts down through the heather and bilberry to the remains of a spoil heap. Bear slightly left here to descend the valley in an area known as Perkin's Beach, an unusual name but probably referring to a pebble laden stream. Another track comes in from the left but you keep right at first then left. Cross a stile and keep ahead on the track as it bends to the right again to run back into the village. Go left for the well earned drink at The Stiperstones.

33. Wentnor

Shropshire Hill walking in a fairly remote part of the county. Several climbs through open countryside.

Distance	6 miles (9.5km)
Allow	3 hours
Map	OS Explorer 216 Welshpool and Montgomery
By bus	The Shropshire Hills shuttle serves Bridges only
By car	Wentnor is signed off the main A489 road between Craven Arms and Lydham. There is a direct road from Shrewsbury (off the A5) by way of Pulverbatch and Bridges to The Green where you turn left for Wentnor. There is a limited amount of car parking in the village
Refreshments	The Crown at Wentnor, the Sun at Norbury and The Inn on The Green
Nearest Tourist Information Office	Shropshire Hills Discovery Centre, Craven Arms Tel: 01588 676000 discovery.centre@shropshire.gov.uk

Wentnor is nestled on a ridge between The Long Mynd and Stiperstones. It is more of a hamlet than village and at one end stands the lovely church dating partly from Norman times, but having been restored extensively during the last century. There is a memorial here to a family who perished under a landslip at The Long Mynd and one or two other features of interest.

1. From the front door of the Crown turn left towards the church and then right downhill but as the road curves right continue ahead along a less steeply graded old green lane. This brings you onto a tarmac road where you turn left to pass by Walkmill. Go over the bridge and in a short distance turn right along a very quiet lane for Norbury.

2. In just less than a mile you meet another road. Go right here into the hamlet of Norbury, with its long standing Sun Inn opposite the church. There is a boulder at the end of the sanctuary said to have been a penance seat in earlier times. Turn right by the telephone kiosk and turn next left. The climb to Linley Hill begins! The road curves right and passes a house. Shortly afterwards, the road climbs more steeply and there is a gateway on the left. Go through here and after a few

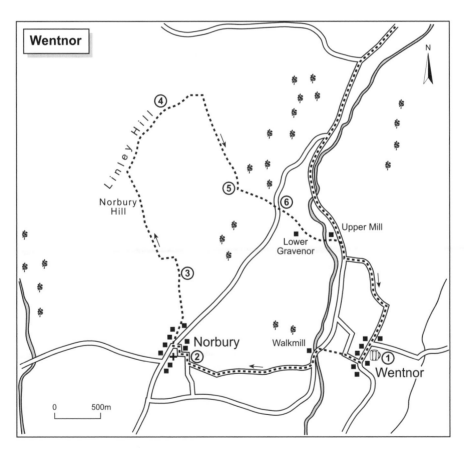

steps go diagonally right across the field to the top right-hand corner. The views are superb but there's more to come. Cross the stile beneath the hazel to re-join the lane.

3. There's no respite. Continue to climb and soon the lane goes over a cattle grid and becomes a bridleway, where you go through a gate and onto a greener section with views over the Stiperstones ahead. Continue along the shoulder of Norbury Hill until you come to the flanks of Linley Hill, renowned for its avenues of beeches planted by the unemployed after the Napoleonic Wars. Go through the gate, the green track bends to a gate with a stile. Cross it and continue ahead with the fence cum hedge on the right. Go through the gateway and continue ahead, still keeping the fence to your right.

4. As you approach the next boundary you might just be able to see the remains of an ancient earthworks to your left. Go over a stile by a gate and walk ahead towards the next field boundary. Cross a stile and walk slightly right to a stile by a gate. Don't cross it. Instead turn right to walk to the corner of the field where you cross a stile into a marshy

Parish church at Norbury

area. You begin to climb following as closely as possible the fence to the left, going through the gateway.

5. As the path begins to descend, keep a look out for stile and a path leading off left towards Lower Gravenor. This follows the fence on the right down the hillside and passes an old quarry scar (be careful here) to a stile beyond. Exit onto a lane. Turn right and then look for a stile on the left

6. Go down the bank keeping ahead to meet a track, above Lower Gravenor Farm. The path runs slightly right down the field to pass to the left of the farm onto the track. Go right here and the track curves around right to the farm but you go through the gate to enter a field on the left. Head slightly right across the field through the remnant hedge (near the electric telegraph pole). Continue in the same direction towards a stile in the bottom corner. Cross this and go over the footbridge. The farm stands to the left but you go right up the track to the road. Cross over to follow the lane, soon on your left, back up to Wentnor village and The Crown Inn. Have you worked up a sufficient thirst?

34. Whitchurch

This walk includes six regional walks and crosses three counties. The other main attraction is the canal locks at Grindley Brook.

Easy walking through meadows and along the Llangollen branch of the Shropshire Union Canal.

Distance	6 miles (10km)
Allow	3-4 hours
Map	OS Explorer 257 Crewe and Nantwich
By train	There is a daily service from Crewe and Shrewsbury
By bus	There are regular buses from Chester and Shrewsbury on Mondays to Saturdays
By car	Whitchurch is on the meeting place of the A41 from the Midlands, the A49 from the South and North and A525 from The Potteries. There are several car parks in town
Refreshments	There are cafés and inns at Whitchurch and Grindley Brook
Nearest Tourist Information Office	St Mary's Street, Whitchurch Tel: 01948 664577

The tall tower of the church stands high above all other buildings in Whitchurch's High Street. This North Shropshire town has several interesting corners and there are several very pleasant Georgian and Victorian frontages throughout the central area.

Whitchurch has always been Shropshire's centre of cheese production and several superb farmhouse cheeses are still produced in the surrounding countryside. Shropshire Blue is a very distinctive cheese made in these parts. Whitchurch is also home to a famous turret clock maker, which you pass on the way into town.

1. Start the walk at Whitchurch railway station. Turn right from the station entrance and walk along the A525 to The Railway public house and cross the main road by way of the pedestrian lights. Continue ahead along Green End, signposted to town centre. This curves right to High Street and Bargates, where the very impressive St Alkmund's church stands to your right. Go left down Yardington, opposite the church, and then turn right into Sherrymill Road. At Waterside Close go right along a path signposted as The Sandstone Trail. This leads to a road at the end of a residential area (by a turning area) where there is a mosaic; this is part of the Mosaic Arts Trail developed by the Whitchurch Walking for Health group in 2008.

   It is interesting to note how much the landscape has changed here in a matter of twenty years. In the first edition (1990) the author noted that there had been '...*development in this area in recent years but a number of small enclosures still remain. It will be interesting to see for how long*'. There has been significant development. To the credit of the planning authority the paths have been retained and some good conservation work done, but I lament the loss of those small pastures.

2. Continue ahead through what is best described as parkland. At the junction of paths keep right to cross Greenfields Rise. Continue ahead by the waymark post, signing your way through the country park. You enter Greenfields Nature Reserve, which is part of the wider Whitchurch Waterway Country Park managed by Shropshire Wildlife Trust. Choose the lower path which runs ahead. It is possible, however, to follow the higher path up the bank and then dip left and down steps to re-join the low level path by a bridge over the stream. Either way, you climb up the bank to the Whitchurch arm of the Llangollen Canal.

3. Turn right and walk on the towpath to cross the lift bridge. Once over go right along the towpath and walk under the first bridge, Number 30 — Danson's Bridge, but then go left, through a kissing gate, to enter a large field.

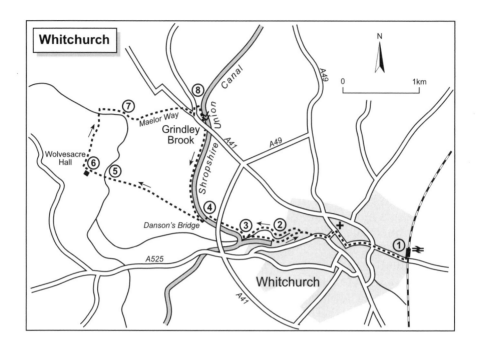

4. Proceed slightly right across this field to a barred gate. Go through it
   and continue in a similar direction. Cross a concrete track and stile
   with numerous waymarker roundels offering a variety of routes to the
   walker. It is also where the Shropshire Way passes. Your way, however,
   is right again towards a field corner where you'll spot a stile by a
   barred gate. Cross it and keep ahead to a barred gate and over another
   concrete track. Keep ahead over undulating ground, possibly the result
   of post glacial deposits. As you approach the strip of woodland ahead,
   look for a small gate (or gateway as the gate was broken when I passed
   by) to the right of two old barred gates, situated in the newer fencing.
   Head down to the stream.

5. Now go through a barred gate and over the bridge then up a bank
   beneath the trees to a gate. Pass to the left of a small pool and skirt
   just to the right of the farm buildings and silage store to reach a stile
   which exits onto a track.

6. Go right along a track lined with oaks. The Maelor Way joins before a
   dwelling. You continue down the dip to a junction. Go right, as

indicated by the way-mark to pass to the right of a dwelling and then to the front of another building to a stile. Please be considerate when passing through. Head slightly right through wet ground to a gateway and then walk slightly left to an eroded bank of the stream. Just along here the path cuts left to a footbridge and stile, leading into the next pasture.

7. Keep ahead with the stream to the right and cross another stile. Walk along the wood's edge to go over a stile (where you are seemingly in Cheshire). Proceed to cross two more stiles and aim for the left of the dwelling. A stile exits on the road — take care as you climb over; traffic moves quite fast even here. Go right and before the junction cross the road by the Horse and Jockey public house.

8. Turn left and at the end of the car park cross the road and walk up the lane, with the garage to your right. The path is signposted as The South Shropshire Way and the Bishop's Bennett Trail also parts company here. At the bridge go right to join the towpath. Climb the flight of locks and pass by the Lockside stores and café. Walk back along the towpath to pass Bridge 30 and onward to the lift bridge, Number 31. Go left to cross it and follow the sandstone trail along the Whitchurch arm to its current terminus and onward to a road. Cross over and go left and then right down steps to re-join the path you used on the outward leg.

It is now a matter of re-tracing your steps back into town and the station.

35. Worfield to Bridgnorth

Gentle walking in the beautiful Worfe valley. There is only one main climb, otherwise the walk is across fields and through woodland. The highlight has to be the tranquility of the Worfe river valley and the old mill at Rindleford.

Distance	5 miles (8km)
Allow	2-3 hours
Map	OS Explorer 218 Wyre Forest and Kidderminster
By bus	There is a daily, mainly hourly service, Bus 890, between Bridgnorth from Wolverhampton. The service is less frequent on Sundays and Bank Holidays. Catch the 890 bus from outside Tesco Express, High Street, Bridgnorth. Ask for The Wheel public house on the main road. There is also a less frequent bus service 114 which runs on Mondays to Saturdays
By car	Bridgnorth is at a hub of several main roads and there is parking near to the Tourist Information Centre in Listley Street
Refreshments	Bridgnorth has many cafes and inns to suit all tastes. There's also the Wheel at the very start of the walk and The Dog (also known as The Davenport Arms) at Worfield, known for its real ale
Nearest Tourist Information Office	The Library, Listley Street, Bridgnorth Tel: 01746 763358

The hillside village of Worfield owes its existence as a bridging point of the River Worfe and has some delightful buildings including the church, the old vicarage (now a hotel) and Lower Hall, a super 16th century half timbered dwelling. Nearby is Davenport House built for Henry Davenport in the early eighteenth century in a baroque style. The walk also passes through the hamlet of Rindleford with the old eighteenth century grain mill which was also used as a cotton mill later in its history. It is now a private residence.

1. Start this linear walk at the bus stop outside Tesco Express in Bridgnorth. Catch the 890 bus service out to Worfield. Ask for The Wheel and the bus stop is opposite the garage just before a junction where you turn left for Worfield village. Keep left at the next junction. Go over Lowe Bridge and ahead to a junction. Turn right if you are visiting The Dog. Otherwise, go left over a stile by a gate.

2. Within 200 metres the path forks. Your way is slightly right up the bank through parkland. Cross the road and climb more steeply in the same direction. To the right is Davenpost House which is not open to the public but is used for social functions. Proceed ahead to pass a waymark post and cross the road again to descend to a stile to the left of a gate. Cross this and head for the bridge over the River Worfe, lined with alders.

3. This is the site of an old mill and the wheel and some of the brickwork still remains; this was evidently used to pump fresh water up to the house. Go right to walk near the river bank but not for long as the path leads slightly left to a stile in the fence. Cross it and head slightly right to the top right corner. Go through a gate and ahead on a track which bends to the left. Aim for a point between the red brick barn and a cottage. Just to the right of the barn is a barred gate. Go through it and cross a stile. You arrive at a junction of paths.

4. Turn right here to pass the cottage and into the wood. You soon exit over a stile and your way is ahead beneath the sandstone scarp slope. Keep left to walk around the corner towards a dwelling. Go left to use the alternative path which climbs a little and then drops down right onto the track in the field. Go left along it, over the bridge and ahead for Rindleford on the track beneath Soudley Rocks.

5. Go through a gate at Rindleford by a dwelling and there stands the old mill on the left, a listed building of some character, and there is a

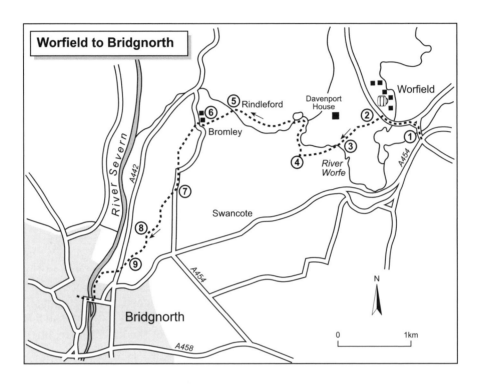

cottage ahead to complete this bucolic setting. However, your way is left here. The pool is to your left and the bridge ahead. As you approach a cottage at the bottom of the hill go right to a paddock where there is a stile almost immediately on the left and ahead to the next stile. Pass to the right of an old engineering building and bear slightly right to a stile leading into a field. Now the climbing begins. Head left up the bank, cross a stile and then go slightly right to rise again beneath a covered reservoir. You will see some houses ahead in Bromley. Aim for the barred gate, where there is a stile next to it. Cross it to join a lane.

6. Go right. As you leave the hamlet, turn left at the corner to go through a gate. Walk ahead in a shallow dry valley and then proceed slightly left. Two paths meet mid-field here and you need to go left to a stile by a tree at the end of a remnant hedge. Cross it and keep ahead to a

brow in a large arable field, where you head slightly left to a gate that exits on to a road. The roads descends to two dwellings.

7. Do not go right up the track but go right over a stile instead to a pasture. A farm stands, to the right, at the top of the field. Head slightly right and through the hedge into the next field and proceed in a similar direction. Go through a gate by a trough at the next boundary and keep ahead to skirt the corner of the wood. Cross a stile and keep ahead. Now, look for a stile on the right into the wood.

8. Go left to keep near to the fence at first. The turn to the right takes you to Jacob's Ladder and High and Pendlestone Rocks, which is great for those who are agile and can cope with heights but perhaps at another time. So, keep left and the path curves to the left and descends, steeply in places. Turn right at the junction and right again to descend between outcrops. This leads to a corralled path which runs alongside the cemetery and drops down steps to the entrance.

9. Go right here to the main road. Turn left and then first right to Severn Park. Walk along the track to the riverside and then turn left to continue ahead by buildings to steps up to the bridge at Lower Town. In my book, this is one of the loveliest ways to enter Bridgnorth as you can really see the spatial layout of Low and High town.

36: Yorton

One of Shropshire's favourite locations, Grinshill hill, with some climbs but mainly easy walking. The highlights of the walk are the superb views, Clive church and the Railway Inn.

Distance	4 miles (6-7km)
Allow	3 hours
Map	OS Explorer 241 Shrewsbury
By train	There is a daily service from Shrewsbury and Crewe. Yorton is a request stop so tell the conductor guard as soon as is possible; you also need to give a signal to the driver when you are on the platform as the train is approaching
By bus	There is a regular bus, 511/13 between Shrewsbury, Wem and Whitchurch calling at Yorton on Mondays to Saturdays
By car	Travel on the A49 to Preston Brockurst where you turn right for Clive and Yorton. There is a limited amount of one street parking
Refreshments	The Railway Inn at Yorton and the Inn at Grinshill both welcome walkers
Nearest Tourist Information Office	Rowley's House, Barker Street Tel: 01743 281200

1. Start from Yorton Railway Station assuming you are travelling from Shrewsbury. On reaching the road, go under the bridge and turn right to walk up the road. Those alighting from the other platform can join here. Pass Yorton Farm and then go left through a barred gate (as signposted). Head slightly left to walk up the field's edge to another

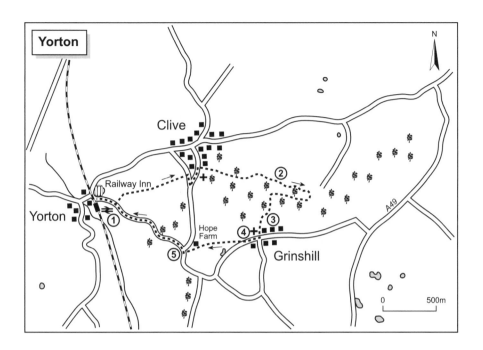

gate. The fields are partitioned for use by horses. Walk ahead in the
next field, alongside the hedge, to a bridle gate. Go through it to join
a track up to the village of Clive. The impressive spire of the church
will guide you. Clive church is a considerable landmark for miles
around. It stands near to Clive Hall dating from Elizabethan times.
Once on the road, go right and this bends to a junction. Go left here to
walk up by the church and take the first right again on a restricted
byway.

2. Walk up the track to Grinshill hill, passing Clive School and the nature
   reserve. The track rises to the summit and runs between woodland and
   fields. Continue until you reach a road. Go right here and then into the
   car park for Corbet Wood. Your way is to the left then the path
   descends to the right beneath the sandstone outcrops. The entire area
   has been subject to quarrying so please keep to the path. At the
   junction keep ahead and at the next one keep left and join a more
   prominent path, which comes in from the left.

3. As you approach the old school keep left. Ahead is the Jubilee Oak planted in 1935 by Miss Cynthia Bibby, sheltering a seat for the weary on their travels! Beyond is a lovely old sandstone track linking a number of houses lying beneath Grinshill Cliff, with splendid views back to Clive Church where you can retrace your steps. That is the short route. However, for those who want a mile or so extra, walk down the lane to a road to exit near to the Inn at Grinshill which welcomes walkers into the bar.

4. Go right along the lane to leave the village. As the road descends look for a stile on the right. Cross this into a field and head slightly right in the direction of the farm. In the next boundary cross the fencing beneath a tree and continue ahead in a similar direction. Cross a stile and now head beyond the farm buildings towards the far right corner, passing to the left of an old tree.

The church at Clive can be seen for miles around

5. Turn right on the road and ahead at the junction. Sansaw is to the left, a classical red brick hall of fine distinction. The lane rises up between sandstone walls and then descends to Yorton railway station and The Railway Inn. I do hope that you have time to adjourn awhile before your train arrives. The entrance is on the side; otherwise you might think it is closed.

New books from Sigma

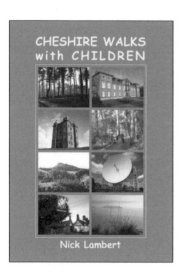

CHESHIRE WALKS WITH CHILDREN 2ND EDITION
Nick Lambert

Now completely revised and updated, this was the first in our "walks with children" series and has quickly become a firm favourite. There are 30 walks, ranging in length, together with things to look out for and questions to answer along the way make it an entertaining book for young and old alike.

£8.99

A SHEPHERD'S LIFE
W H Hudson

This classic narrative of rural life in the late 1800s transports the reader to the vast downs of the Salisbury Plain. It vividly captures life at that time and place, covering every subject related to a shepherd's work and life, from his beloved sheep dog, to the local landowner.

£9.99

THE CHARLIE CHAPLIN WALK
Stephen P Smith

Explore the London streets of Charlie Chaplin's childhood in a chronological tour that can be taken on foot or from the comfort of an armchair. This book concentrates on the story of Chaplin's formative years and takes a fresh look at the influence they had upon his films.

£9.99

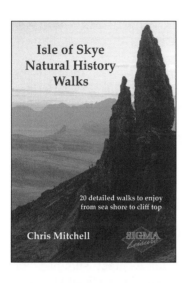

ISLE OF SKYE NATURAL HISTORY WALKS

20 detailed walks to enjoy from sea shore to cliff top

Chris Mitchell

An alternative guide to the wildlife and geology of Skye detailing where to see the island's lesser-known natural history. There are 20 walks based around Portree, Dunvegan, Broadford and Sleat together with detailed maps and quality photographs.
£9.99

Available 31st March 2010

ALL-TERRAIN PUSHCHAIR WALKS: LANCASHIRE

Kathryn Wood

30 graded walks from level routes on high fells and wild open moorland, ancient woodlands and forestry plantations, delightful riverside rambles and bracing coastal paths
£7.99

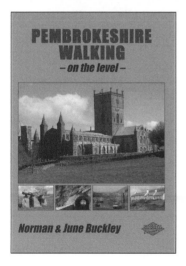

PEMBROKESHIRE WALKING

On the level

Norman & June Buckley

Discover both the breath-taking splendour of the Pembrokeshire coast and its diverse inland landscape. The 25 walks in this book include a brief description of features encountered along the way as well as recommendations for refreshment.
£8.99

Available 30th April 2010

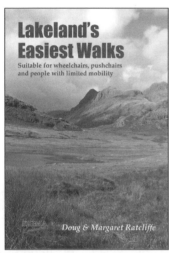